SOS SOBRIETY

SOS

SOBRIETY

MORE SUCCESSFUL THAN AA!

The Proven
Alternative
to 12-step
Programs

BY JAMES CHRISTOPHER
founder of the
Save Our Selves Movement

PROMETHEUS BOOKS
BUFFALO, NY

Published 1992 by Prometheus Books

96 95 94 93 92   5 4 3 2 1

Library of Congress Cataloging-in-Publication Data

Christopher, James, 1942–
    SOS sobriety : the proven alternative to 12-step programs / by James Christopher.
        p.   cm.
    Includes bibliographical references.
    ISBN 0-87975-726-4
    1. Secular Organizations for Sobriety. 2. Alcoholics—Rehabilitation. 3. Alcoholism—Physiological aspects. 4. Alcoholics—Rehabilitation—United States. I. Title. II. Title: SOS sobriety.
HV5278.C47   1992
362.29′286—dc20   92-7772
                                                            CIP

Printed in Canada on acid-free paper.

Contents

Acknowledgments

The material presented in this book is the result of thousands of hours of work and an international collective effort by SOS members and their respective families and friends, dedicated treatment professionals, and distinguished academic research teams.

I would like to thank some of these contributors by name: Dr. Gerard J. Connors, Dr. Kurt H. Dermen, and Mark Duerr of the Research Institute on Addictions; Dr. William M. London, Karen E. Courchaine, and David L. Yoho with the Graduate School of Education, Kent State University; Dr. Kenneth Blum, Professor, Department of Pharmacology, the University of Texas Health Sciences Center; Dr. P. Joseph Frawley, Medical Director, Schick Shadel Hospital; Alana Bowman, Supervising Deputy City Attorney, Los Angeles, California; Thomas Flynn, Executive Director, Inquiry Media Productions; Timothy Madigan, Executive Editor, *Free Inquiry* magazine; Susan E. Smith; Rosalind Gold, Esq.; James L. Monroe, Esq.; Richard Smith; John Lanagan; and Betty Zavon, R.N. Thanks also to Ranjit Sandhu, for hundreds of hours of transcriptions; Larry Beck; Thomas Hill; Brent Bailey and Stephen DiDonna for tireless efforts in typewritten copy; and Carl Schultz for his fine artwork. Special thanks to Dr. Paul Kurtz, publisher of Prometheus Books, for his long-standing support and vision, and to Barbara Bergstrom, editor extraordinaire, for her talent, insight, and encouragement.

7

Introduction

This is a book about the SOS (Secular Organizations for Sobriety; Save Our Selves) abstinence–human support movement and its effective self-empowerment method for achieving and maintaining a lasting sobriety: the Sobriety Priority Program. Thousands of alcoholics and addicts have achieved and maintained sobriety in SOS, thousands who could not do so in other programs.

What, then, are these "other programs"? The vast majority of them are based upon the 12 steps of Alcoholics Anonymous (AA). These 12 "spiritual" steps constitute the basic program of AA and its derivatives—i.e., Narcotics Anonymous; Cocaine Anonymous; Overeaters Anonymous; Gamblers Anonymous; Alanon, Alateen, Alatot (12-step programs for families and friends of alcoholics and addicts); Adult Children of Alcoholics; co-dependency groups, etc. This plethora of programs seems to offer all one could ask for in "recovery." At close range, however, the core "program" is the same. The culprit behind these addictions, we are told, is a "spiritual" malady involving "character defects."

Alcoholics Anonymous's 12 "spiritual" steps—an approach that many perceive as a shame-based program that promotes "learned helplessness"—has indeed helped thousands of alcoholics achieve sobriety. To suggest, though, that a 12 "spiritual" step program helps everyone is false.

9

No human being ever intends to get hooked. Many persons (i.e., nonalcoholics) can ingest alcohol moderately—even heavily, it seems—with impunity. Others get hooked on alcohol, even though both types may all drink together for the same reasons. Why do some become alcoholics while others do not? The jury is still out, but it is approaching a decision. Meanwhile, consider this: Anyone who drinks alcohol comes, to some degree, "under the influence." The majority, however, don't become alcoholics. Do these people possess an especially strong character—character that cannot be compromised via chemically altered states? And what of the other mind-altering drugs: e.g., cocaine, heroin, methamphetamines? It has been well established that these drugs are not "selectively addictive," as is alcohol; virtually all who use these drugs get hooked eventually. Our "lizard brains" or primitive limbic systems know nothing of character or resolve.

Blakiston's *Gould Medical Dictionary* (third edition) defines the "limbic system" as follows:

> A ring of cerebral cortex . . . the oldest portion of the cortex which has its evolutionary rudiment in the reptiles, amphibians, and fish. Now thought to control various emotional and behavioral patterns.

It is crucial to note that there is no apparent need for support groups for folks who continually thrust their hands into a roaring fire. Our limbic system imprints of "fire = pain" control this automatically for virtually all living organisms.

Having experienced chemical addiction at the cellular level for seventeen years, I *compensate* for my polluted primitive limbic system or "lizard brain," which contains countless thousands of "alcohol = pleasure" imprints. I *compensate* for my human selective-memory "alcohol = pleasures" associations by "manually" maintaining the awareness that, for me, the ingestion of alcohol/drugs = *pain,* perhaps not instantly but ultimately. For me sobriety = survival.

In sobriety I have the potential to experience a quality of life, i.e., "recovery," *as a separate issue* from my Sobriety Priority.

This "recovery" is based upon my personal expectations, my genetic limitations, and the realization of my realistic human potentials, factoring in the uncertainties of life circumstances.

Yes, Virginia, there are victims. As I stated earlier, no human being ever intended to get hooked. There are soundrels, rascals, and just plain folks; heroes, heroines, and others; each consciously "doing sobriety" as a "cut-to-the-chase" survival necessity choice, *as a separate issue*—like a diabetic who acknowledges and accepts his or her diabetes and prioritizes his or her survival necessity to take insulin and maintain a dietary regimen as an issue separate from all else. The diabetic does this deliberately regardless of his or her human tendency toward denial (via wishful thinking or selective memory); regardless of pleasurable or negative life circumstances, human angst, pleasurable or negative feelings. The diabetic best not become complacent regarding his or her requirement for insulin and a dietary plan.

As a sober alcoholic I cannot drink alcohol (or ingest other mind-altering drugs) and get away with it; I cannot drink or use with impunity. Religious or nonreligious, black or white, male or female, the diabetic had better take insulin, the alcoholic maintain the Sobriety Priority as a separate issue aside from all else.

Then could the focus of 12-step groups be skewed? Clearly there is a need for alternatives and options in "recovery." Women for Sobriety, with its "thirteen statements of acceptance," offers an empowerment approach and the rebuilding of self-esteem through its New Life Program. And more recently, Charlotte Davis Kasl, in her new book *Many Roads, One Journey: Moving Beyond the Twelve Steps,* provides a 16-step empowerment model.

Rational Recovery (RR) utilizes Albert Ellis's Rational Emotive Therapy (RET), viewing "heavy drinking" as a behavior, dismissing as "not helpful" research on the physiological components of alcoholism. Rational Recovery meetings are currently held at no cost, as I understand it; however, professional therapists are present with business cards at the ready. That is the nature of the beast. RET shrinks sooner or later reap the benefits of their guidance via a stream of new clients.

Rational Recovery, in my view, clearly waffles on the abstinence issue. SOS does not. AA does not. Women for Sobriety does not. Case in point: A few days ago, an SOS member, sober for more than three years, called RR headquarters in Lotus, California. A pleasant female voice answered his general queries. He relates the incident as follows:

"Jim, I'm fuming over this! When I spoke to this woman she explained the RR method to be like a 'cure,' that is, after attending RR professionally led group meetings once a week from six months to a year, apparently at no cost (although a professional therapist is available for additional one-on-one counseling), she said members were encouraged to leave the group as fully recovered, and that a return to 'controlled drinking' was a reasonable outcome for some.

"Jim, I know what my reaction to her message would have been if I had made that call to RR in my early sobriety. As with any person new to recovery, shaky and desperate and vulnerable, I would have zeroed in on 'We find that a return to controlled drinking is a reasonable outcome for some.' This is a very seductive message to people new to recovery. Like any alcoholic in early sobriety I would have loved to hear it! And it would have killed me!"

It may be well that within the SOS freethought forum for recovery one may also choose outside therapy, the utilization of AA's 12 steps, Women for Sobriety's thirteen statements of acceptance, the tenets of secular humanism, Buddhism, Christianity, etc. But, long-term sobrietists tend to maintain their sobriety as a separate issue, individually choosing their own quality-of-life program.

When the chemical-dependency treatment industry will at long last offer a "dual diagnosis" model for all, allowing focus on sobri-ety as a separate issue, and when treatment professionals will cease to tell folks how to live via spiritual or secular dogma, we will open the door to multiple options in the recovery field.

This book, then, is not a shame-based "spiritual" chronicle, negating reason; nor is it a glib scientistic parody, claiming rational-ity yet negating reams of scientific research regarding genetic and physiological components of alcoholism and drug addiction. This is a book that does not blame the victim, spiritually or secularly. This is a book that covers the evolution of SOS from its first meeting to the present day, including anonymous SOS recovery stories and the results of two scientific studies that utilized a random-selection process involving thousands of SOS members.

The Alternative

1. The SOS Story: Questions and Answers

Q: What is alcoholism, anyway?

A: The jury is still out. Personally, I'm impressed by the reams of research data that show some folks (about 10 percent of this country's populace) become physiologically hooked on booze at the cellular level, experiencing (over time) problems in their lives directly attributed to ingesting the drug alcohol. Incidentally, I've never met anyone who intended to get hooked on alcohol or any other drug. Other people, i.e., nonalcoholics, seem to be able to drink as they choose, when they choose, with impunity. Some of us seem to be predestined to cellular addiction via genetics; some researchers also include the possibility that any drinker —who consumes alcohol long enough and hard enough—may eventually join the "cellular addiction crowd." This means that one's primitive limbic system, or the "lizard brain," that knows only its need, receives an alcohol = pleasure imprint with each sip of booze, regardless of the next morning's hangover, smashed car, or wrecked life. Most SOS members are comfortable with viewing alcoholism as both a progressive disease process and a habit, but SOS meetings offer a "freethought forum for recovery." Therefore, if anyone were to attend an SOS meeting expressing a desire to achieve and maintain sobriety (abstinence) by a differ-

17

ent pathway, he or she would be welcome. Even if a person stated that he or she stayed sober by jumping on a trampoline twice a day, he or she would be welcomed.

Q: That's cute, but what about those persons who wish to learn to control and enjoy their drinking? Does SOS accommodate them?

A: No. Their needs would be better served elsewhere. Our name says it all: *Secular Organizations for Sobriety* and *Save Our Selves*. We're an *abstinence* group. Anyone sincerely seeking sobriety in a secular setting is welcome.

Q: It's obvious from your personal story and from your writings that you are a secular or nonreligious person and that you founded SOS on that basis. What about religious or "spiritual" persons? What about persons with chemical addictions and problems other than alcohol? Does SOS accommodate them as well?

A: Since its beginnings with the first SOS meeting in November 1986, SOS (then called SSG, or Secular Sobriety Groups) welcomed *anyone* sincerely seeking sobriety in a secular setting. Like most self-help support groups, we tried to convey in our name what we were about. Many of the more "heretical" members, including myself, thought that religious persons would not want to attend our meetings, although one need not be a secular person to attend a secular meeting, e.g., support groups for cancer patients, AIDS victims, etc. Still, we thought that the recovery needs of religious persons were being met quite well, thank you, in the readily available 12-step groups, namely AA and its derivatives (CA, NA, OA, etc.). But, as I stated, from the very first SOS meeting ever held we welcomed the attendance of religious as well as nonreligious persons. Some of us "heretics" initially joked and jousted, tossing about our nonreligious viewpoints, thrilled at last to be in the company of others who shared similar perspectives on life. We realized, however, that human life was at stake, and when persons not sharing these views started attending SOS meetings and took offense at inappropriate nonreligious remarks, members "bent over backwards" to make the religious persons feel at home. You see, many of us had not felt at home in AA with its 12 "spiritual" steps, its "program" for living. But it has been my experience that —although no gathering of *Homo sapiens* is perfect—SOS groups seem to convey more respect for "you-as-you-are" than do the 12-step groups.

I believe this phenomenon has a lot to do with our premise, our "structure," if you will. Yes, we welcome *all* who seek recovery from alcoholism and freedom from addiction to drugs other than alcohol (cocaine, methamphetamines, heroin, etc.); persons with problems regarding overeating, gambling, smoking, etc.; and families and friends of alcoholics and addicts. We attempt to provide a safe, secular (not anti-religious) environment in which we can "Save Our Selves" by achieving and maintaining sobriety/ abstinence/recovery while supporting each other in the process, as life's problems do not have to be faced alone.

Q: Okay. Religious persons as well as nonreligious persons are welcome to attend SOS, but why wouldn't religious persons prefer the AA model?

A: Many do and many don't. Religious SOS members tell us: "God helps those who help themselves," or "I want a separation of church and recovery," or "I already have a religion, so I don't need another." Many religious persons attend SOS instead of 12-step groups, crediting *themselves* with their individual personal achievement of sobriety, and thus empowering themselves to continue to stay sober. Our approach tends to help foster, nurture, and rebuild self-esteem, self-reliance, self-determination, and a healthy ego. SOS members prefer the experience of an "internal locus of control" to the passivity of giving full credit to something or someone else. We credit ourselves for our achievement and maintenance of sobriety as a separate issue from all else, including religious or "spiritual" beliefs. In short, we are happy for human support, but no one can crawl inside us to keep us sober. Mainstream Christians, Jews, Buddhists, and others feel "liberated" in a freethought secular setting, as do agnostics, rationalists, and skeptics. We're not out to convert, recruit, or blast one another. We thrive in an atmosphere of diversity, recovery, and change, rather than wallow in "learned helplessness."

Q: Are you saying that AA promotes "learned helplessness"?

A: AA was founded in 1935 by Bill Wilson, an ex-stockbroker, and Dr. Bob Smith, a physician—both alcoholics—as an offshoot of the Oxford Group, which was founded by Dr. Frank Buchman, an evangelical Protestant theologian. "Bill W." and "Dr. Bob" practiced the Oxford Group's precepts. The "alcoholic squadron" members of the Oxford Group formally broke off to begin Alcoholics Anonymous in 1938 and in 1939 published the AA "Big Book" with its 12 "spiritual" steps, a distillation of Oxford Group principles. In answer to your question, I offer the "heart" of the AA program.

Without help [our alcoholism] is too much for us. But there is One who has all power—that One is God. May you find Him now!

Half measures availed us nothing. We stood at the turning point. We asked His protection and care with complete abandon.

Here are the steps we took, which are suggested as a program of recovery:

1. We admitted we were powerless over alcohol—that our lives had become unmanageable.
2. Came to believe that a Power greater than ourselves could restore us to sanity.
3. Made a decision to turn our will and our lives over to the care of God as we understood Him.
4. Made a searching and fearless moral inventory of ourselves.
5. Admitted to God, to ourselves, and to another human being the exact nature of our wrongs.
6. Were entirely ready to have God remove all these defects of character.

7. Humbly asked him to remove our shortcomings.
8. Made a list of all persons we had harmed, and became willing to make amends to them all.
9. Made direct amends to such people whenever possible, except when to do so would injure them or others.
10. Continued to take personal inventory and when we were wrong promptly admitted it.
11. Sought through prayer and meditation to improve our conscious contact with God as we understood Him, praying only for knowledge of His will for us and the power to carry that out.
12. Having had a spiritual awakening as the result of these steps, we tried to carry this message to alcoholics, and to practice these principles in all our affairs . . . our personal adventures before and after make clear three pertinent ideas:

    (a) That we were alcoholic and could not manage our own lives.
    (b) That probably no human power could have relieved our alcoholism.
    (c) That God could and would if He were sought.[1]

Q: Is SOS anti-AA? Haven't countless thousands been helped by its program?

A: Any persons who want to get and stay sober (i.e., recover) from alcohol or any other drug addiction, or to apply the SOS approach to other issues threatening their lives and/or quality of life, are welcome to attend SOS, including members of other groups. SOS respects recovery however it may be achieved. Some of our members, within a freethought setting, have expressed anti-AA sentiments via their perception of AA as having been touted as "the only effective way to recovery." I have found most SOS members are glad about AA "being there." We should not overlook the fact that we need alternatives. *One size does not fit all.* Diversity demands diversity.

Yes, AA has helped countless thousands, but it has also failed countless thousands as well. Twelve "spiritual" steps, or "stepomania" as some critics have called the AA program, is not the only way. SOS offers another approach, an approach that has been utilized succesfully by thousands to date, thousands who could not recover in AA.

Q: It sounds as though SOS was born out of frustration with the existing 12-step programs. Is that the case?

A: Yes. I firmly believe in the effectiveness of a "separation of church and recovery." Nonreligious persons have died of alcohol and other chemical addictions because they could not perform AA's "mental gymnastics." They failed in their attempts to retranslate or rework "spiritual" design-for-living steps. Adherents to any "one true way" approach may say "whatever works is fine," but in practice they can be nonsupportive and mean-spirited toward detractors who dare to dissent. And religious or "spiritual" persons oftentimes prefer to worship in their own church or synagogue.

I had been sober for a number of years (my sobriety date is April 24, 1978) when I wrote of my frustrations concerning AA. Some of the people who responded had been sober many years but had left AA early in their sobriety out of frustration, as I had. Yes, we maintained our sobriety, but we missed the empathy, warmth, compassion, and understanding that a self-help "common cause" support group could provide. And persons who desperately wanted to achieve sobriety had written, virtually pleading for alternatives to AA. I wrote more articles and gave talks. One woman drove over forty miles to attend one of my talks. She had been sober for a number of years, but she missed self-help support group interaction. I convened the first SOS group shortly after that talk, because that lady had strongly suggested that someone should start such a group. Many new movements are born out of frustration at unmet needs.

Q: Does SOS then define itself by what it is not, rather than by what it is?

A: Our reason for being, born out of frustration with the lack of options in recovery, has evolved to state more clearly what we are rather than what we are not, but comparisons to AA are inevitable. AA has been around for almost sixty years; it has been "where those alcoholics go" for so long in the minds of most people that alternatives are virtually unknown. That, happily, is changing. We *are* a secular self-help support network of groups. We *are* an abstinence program. We *are* a program of self-empowerment. We *are* a freethought forum for recovery.

Q: What is the SOS program of recovery?

A: The SOS "program" is offered as a suggested strategy. It will help you achieve and maintain a lasting, continual abstinence-freedom from alcohol and drug dependency. Persons grappling with issues other than alcoholism (overeaters, gamblers, etc.) have successfully utilized the SOS approach as well. Here's the essence of the SOS program.

The Cycle of Addiction

The Sobriety Priority approach for achieving and maintaining freedom from alcohol and other mind-altering drugs is a *cognitive* strategy. It can be applied on a daily basis to prevent relapse as long as one lives.

The Sobriety Priority approach respects the power of "nature" (genetic inheritance, progressive disease processes) and of "nurture" (learned habit, behaviors,and asssociations) by showing how to achieve the initial arrest of cellular addiction and stave off the chronic habits that result from this addiction.

The "cycle of addiction" (see Figure 1) contains three debilitating elements: chemical need (at the physiological cellular level), learned habit (chronic, drinking/using behaviors and associations), and denial of both need and habit.

Figure 1. The Cycle of Addiction

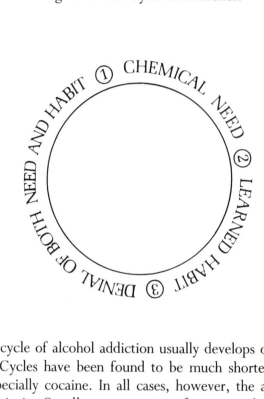

The cycle of alcohol addiction usually develops over a period of years. Cycles have been found to be much shorter with other drugs, especially cocaine. In all cases, however, the addiction becomes "Priority One," a separate issue from everything else. And as the addiction progresses, it begins to negate everything else.

The Cycle of Sobriety

The cycle of addiction can be successfully replaced by another cycle: the cycle of sobriety (see Figure 2). This cycle contains three essential elements: acknowledgment of one's addiction to alcohol or drugs (perhaps once euphemistically called "a problem"), acceptance of one's disease/habit, and prioritization of sobriety as the primary issue in one's life.

The daily cognitive application of a new "Priority One," the Sobriety Priorty, as a separate issue arrests the cycle of addiction.

It frees the sober alcoholic/addict to experience "everything else" by teaching him or her to associate "everything else" with sobriety, not with drinking or using behaviors. The cycle of sobriety remains in place only so long as the sober alcoholic/addict cognitively chooses to continue to acknowledge the existence of his or her alcoholism or drug addiction.

The Sobriety Priority, applied daily, gradually weakens booze and drug associations, halting the cycle of addiction and allowing time for new associations to form as one experiences life without addictive chemicals. As one continues to "make peace" with the facts regarding his or her arrested addiction—that is, as one continues to recognize alcohol and/or drugs as *non*options—one comes to prefer a sober lifestyle: one longs to preserve it, to respect the arrested chemical addiction, and to protect the new, sober life.[2]

Figure 2. The Cycle of Sobriety

Q: Is SOS, then, focusing on achieving and maintaining sobriety (i.e., abstinence) rather than a "wholistic" recovery?

A: Yes. SOS members can utilize "the sobriety priority" as a separate issue from all else, so that in sobriety they are then "freed up" to address their other life issues.

Q: Yes, but where's the "program" as it pertains to a plan for living?

A: The Sobriety Priority, accepted and maintained as a separate issue, empowers one to choose his or her own plan or design for living, regardless of one's unresolved life issues. *We deliberately offer no quality-of-life program: We do not tell each other how to live.* Consequently, we eschew sponsorship (the AA "buddy system") because it has been shown to foster "guruism." Instead, we approach each other as equals, respecting our diversity.

Q: What about one's reasons for drinking in the first place? How is that addressed?

A: Research has shown that alcoholics and nonalcoholics drink for the same reasons. Some will get hooked, others will not (so much for the "alcoholic personality" theories). One's original reasons for drinking may have dissipated over time or may remain in full force. But, if one has acknowledged and accepted the fact that one cannot drink and get away with it, and if one maintains awareness of that fact as a required life-and-death necessity, one has no real choice. Therefore, drinking is not an option when one's survival is seriously threatened. I cannot escape life's challenges by walking in front of an oncoming bus without paying the ultimate price—i.e., I cannot walk in front of an oncoming bus and get away with it. My "lizard brain" or limbic system reacts instantly to "flight or fight"/"do or don't" survival situations.

Sips of alcohol imprint on the limbic system as instantaneous pleasure, not pain. Sticking one's hand in a flame imprints as instantaneous pain. So one automatically avoids this behavior in the future. Alcohol avoidance can become immediate if a person accepts that alcohol literally threatens his or her survival. A person's recognition of his or her survival needs thereby can compensate for that person's natural selective memory and negate denial. Rather than resolving issues that may have been one's original reason(s) to drink, rather than attempting to live in a certain way to avoid certain human emotions or circumstances any human being is likely to experience, one can choose to stay sober and to avoid alcohol "no matter what"—*because no reason in the universe exists for a drink if one acknowledges and accepts that it threatens one's very survival.* For alcoholics drink = pain, or drink = death. Survival is at stake. Therefore, limbic system lies are challenged by passionate realizations of truth: "My name is Jim. I am a sober alcoholic. I cannot and do not drink no matter what, because I cannot drink and get away with it." This is not a statement about my "character." Rather, it is an acknowledgement and acceptance of truth regarding me, physiologically, chemically. *A separate issue.* My survival depends upon it.

Q: So you're staying sober as a separate issue, prioritizing and protecting your sobriety as your number-one life issue by maintaining your awareness that you cannot drink (or use, if you're addicted to other drugs?) How do you deal with unresolved issues?

A: Let me clarify my personal position and the general position of SOS members at large regarding drug addictions other than—or as well as—alcoholism. We choose "across-the-board sobriety" in recovery. I would be at risk experimenting with other mind-altering drugs (1) because of the rather well-established "cross-tolerance" theories (i.e., addiction to one mind-altering drug might well predispose one to become addicted to another mind-altering drug); and (2) the influence of a mind-altering drug weakens anyone's (alcoholic or nonalcoholic) ability to choose, to maintain an awareness of one's real situation.

How do we deal with unresolved issues? Like most people, we (now being free to get on with our lives) can choose to work on certain aspects of ourselves that we'd like to change, perhaps with the aid of professional counseling, secular or spiritual; perhaps by way of returning to school or college, reading and exploring any of a number of fresh options. Recovering people—all people, really—are generally doing the best they can, moving at their own pace through life. In SOS, as we achieve and maintain sobriety, we tend to grow individually. Some issues in one's life may never come to a resolution. Knowing how to "do sobriety" as a protected separate issue does guarantee an end to alcohol- (or other drug-) related problems; it does not guarantee that unrelated life circumstances will change without work—sometimes hard work. I pick an extreme example. Recently, a prominent nonalcoholic radio shrink fatally shot himself, perhaps due to a court case pending (as the media revealed) the next day after I'd appeared on his talk show. Obviously, life can be difficult. Folks may do their best, but tragedy can occur.

The Deputy City Attorney of Los Angeles, Domestic Violence Unit, has told me that violent behavior, with *or without* the involvement of alcohol and drugs, occurs with alarming frequency. We find out who we are in sobriety. In some cases, unwanted behaviors stop in sobriety; in other cases they do not. Perhaps alcohol was only a mask, not the cause. SOS is not advocating "scoundrelism." We simply respect diversity. Obviously, one should obey the laws of the land, as society as we know it requires protection. Also, societal inequalities can cause some people to turn to alcohol and other drugs. These societal ills should be vigorously addressed as a separate issue. Prevention through education can generally be extremely effective. An excellent example is this country's effective programs of education that reveal in a straightforward manner the dangers of tobacco use. Let folks know what they're in for and many will make wise choices.

Q: How are SOS meetings conducted? What happens? What are the "healing dynamics" within this "freethought forum in recovery"?

A: I contend that the very act of people sharing together is an acknowledgement of one's situation. Bolstered by the empathic support of one's peers, freethought-forum, egalitarian self-help groups can be "dynamite" in positive effectiveness! When your meeting format provides a focus, factoring out rigid contols (and controllers), "spiritual" or secular, you can really get somewhere. You can experience positive change and growth.

I am not the first person to hold these ideas. Jeffrey Masson, formerly a prominent practicing psychoanalyst and projects director of the Sigmund Freud Archives, states in the preface to his controversial book *Against Therapy: Emotional Tyranny and the Myth of Psychological Healing:* "I have some ideas about how people could live without psychotherapy or psychiatry. I am thinking of self-help groups that are leaderless and avoid authoritarian structures, in which no money is exchanged, that are not grounded on religious principles (a difficulty with Alcoholics Anonymous and similar groups, since not all members share spiritual or religious interests), and in which all participants have experienced the problem they come to discuss."[3]

Q: SOS, then, offers a way, not "the way." What about other alternatives to 12-step groups that are now coming to the fore? What about research and popular books concerning alcoholics achieving "moderation"?

A: Addressing alcoholism as a physiological disease process and a habit, we feel, makes more sense than self-flagellation over "character defects" in 12-step "spiritual" groups, or in rigid "rational" approaches with shrinks looming in the background, business cards at the ready. Human beings are neither worms nor computers.

One alternative group has begun offering an abstinence alternative for nonreligious people, evolving to offer both abstinence and moderation options. Another new group, backed by shrinks, sees "heavy drinking" primarily as a *behavior;* thus moderation is held out as an option "for some people."

Several books by "authority figures" extend the possibility of achieving moderation for "heavy drinkers." I offer here the scientific conclusions regarding the "controlled drinking" controversy, extensively quoted from the text of *Alcohol and the Addictive Brain,* a new book written by Dr. Kenneth Blum, Ph.D., in collaboration with James E. Payne.*

"Forty years of research into the causes of alcoholism and other addictions have led to one conclusion: Irresistible craving is a malfunction of the reward centers of the brain involving the neurotransmitters and the enzymes that control them. Genetic research . . . indicates that the malfunction begins in the gene. Psychological and sociological research indicates that the environment can trigger, worsen, or to some degree alleviate the genetic predisposition, but the determining factors are biogenetic and biochemical.

"The Controversy over 'Controlled Drinking'

"There are, of course, those who disagree. Indeed, a replay of an old controversy about the underlying nature of alcoholism is now under way. On one side are the scientists whose work I have described in this book. We hold, and I submit, have demonstrated that alcoholism is a biogenetic disease characerized by genetic anomalies leading to biochemical deficiencies or imbalances, and receptor malfunctions.

"On the other side are a few psychologists and a philosopher, who ignore the vast body of research findings over the past four decades, reject the great mass of clinical data, reject even the disease concept, and advance three misleading hypotheses. In my view, these hypotheses are based on insufficient scientific knowledge, or misinterpetations, or on data compiled without true scientific rigor.

"*Hypothesis One.* Total abstinence from alcohol and other psychoactive drugs is not necessary for recovery.

---

*Quoted with the permission of the publisher.

"The Davies Report

"This hypothesis seems to have been derived, in part, from an early experiment in 1962 by D. L. Davies, who studied "normal drinking in recovered alcohol addicts." His findings were cited in the *American Psychologist* in 1983 by Alan Marlatt at the University of Seattle:

> 'Over two decades ago, Davies sent shock waves through the alcoholism field by publishing the result of a long-term follow-up of patients treated for alcoholism at the Maudsley Hospital in London. In his report, Davies (1961) challenged the traditional emphasis on total abstinence as the only viable "cure" for alcoholism by showing that of 93 male alcoholics who were followed up for a period of from 7 to 11 years after treatment, 7 reported a pattern of normal drinking.'

"One problem with Marlatt's interpretation of this study is that it ignores the stated fact that seven out of 93 subjects is less than 8 percent, a tiny fraction. Furthermore, he seems to have overlooked Davies' own final conclusion at the end of his report: 'It is suggested that such cases are more common than has hitherto been recognized, and that the generally accepted view that no alcohol addict can ever again drink normally should be modified, *although all patients should be advised to aim at total abstinence*' [Italics mine].

"The Griffith Edwards Report

"The most important fallacy behind these data was revealed in 1985 when Griffith Edwards reported a follow-up study—three decades later—of the seven subjects in Davies' sample who were supposed to have been able to drink normally. Edwards found that of the seven alcoholic men, five had resumed destructive drinking patterns; three of the five at some time had also used psychoactive drugs heavily; and three of the five had been using alcohol abnormally even during Davies' study. One of the seven eventually experienced Wernicke-Korsakoff syndrome, a form of alcohol-related brain damage; one was hospitalized for peptic ulcers; and one experienced liver enlargement as a result of heavy drinking.

"The data in support of controlled drinking have a way of disintegrating when they are examined closely.

"*Hypothesis Two.* Alcoholism is not a disease, but merely a pattern of learned behavior.

"The Sobells' Report

"This hypothesis was derived largely from the much-publicized work of Mark and Linda Sobell at Patton State Hospital in the California Department of Mental Hygiene in Patton, California. They attempted to prove that alcoholics could be *taught* controlled drinking skills, and that these skills would be effective outside the hospital environment. Again, the underlying thesis was that abstinence is not essential to recovery. The Sobells reported on a group of 20 alcoholic patients who had received behavioral therapy aimed at moderating their drinking patterns. In a follow-up study lasting two years, they claimed that 19 of the patients were successfully practicing controlled drinking.

"One of the leading proponents of the idea of controlled drinking is Herbert H. Fingarette in the Department of Philosophy at the University of California in Santa Barbara. In his book *Heavy Drinking: The Myth of Alcoholism as a Disease,* he referred to the Sobells' work in the following words, 'In 1973, Mark Sobell and Linda Sobell issued their groundbreaking report detailing the successful result of their elaborate and carefully evaluated program of controlled drinking.' Summing up his own views on the subject, he said, 'Controlled drinking has become the umbrella term for the notion that abstinence may not be the only reasonable goal for the heavy drinker seeking help.'

"Unfortunately for the proponents of controlled drinking, the Sobells' work did not stand up to closer scrutiny. On July 9, 1982,

Science published a ten-year follow-up of the Sobells' evidence by M. L. Pendery, I. M. Maltzman, and L. J. West in the Department of Psychiatry at UCLA. The study showed that 13 of the 20 Sobell subjects were hospitalized again within a year, and three others had used alcohol destructively during the period of the study. The other four subjects were found to be psychologically, though not physically, dependent on alcohol. Of these four, three had a record of repetitive arrests on drunk charges. Only one of them seemed to be able to indulge in controlled drinking, and this individual may not have been properly classed as an alcoholic. By 1983, five of the 20 subjects had suffered alcohol-related deaths—one-fourth of the sample. All were under the age of 42 at the time of death.

"*Hypothesis Three.* Alcoholism can be arrested, and often cured.

"The Rand Reports

"To test this hypothesis, among others, the Rand Corporation, under contract from NIAAA, carried out two studies of alcoholics, one in 1976, and one in 1981. The first report evaluated 597 alcoholics 18 months after they had completed treatment. The authors found that 24 percent were abstaining, and 22 percent were drinking normally.

"This report was greeted with pleasure by adherents of the controlled drinking doctrine. For example, Morris Chafetz, former director of NIAAA, stated: 'The Rand Report should make those interested in the plight of alcoholic people jump for joy.' Samuel B. Guze, head of the Department of Psychiatry at the Washington University School of Medicine, said: 'What the data demonstrate is that remission is possible in many alcoholics, and that many of these are able to drink normally for an extended period.'

"But the research methodology and conclusions of the first Rand Report were considered highly suspect by major scientists in the field. For two examples:

"Ernest Noble, at that time director of the NIAAA, was particularly concerned about the effect of the Report on alcoholics and on the treatment community:

'Until further definite scientific evidence exists to the contrary . . . I feel that abstinence must continue as the appropriate goal in the treatment of alcoholism. Furthermore, it
would be extremly unwise for a recovered alcoholic to even
try to experiment with controlled drinking.'

"John Wallace, currently president of the Edgehill-Newport
alcoholism treatment center, commented:

'The First Rand Report was so methodologically inadequate
that nothing could be concluded from it. . . . The report
was seriously marred by an enormous "lost to follow-up"
rate, sample bias on outcome, unreliable and invalid measurement of quality and frequency of consumption, loss of
entire treatment centers from the original sample of centers,
shoddy data-gathering procedures by treatment staff, and a
follow-up window of such short duration (30 days of drinking behaivor) that it was an embarrassment.'

"When the Second Rand Report was released, it claimed nearly
40 percent of the subjects were drinking normally after four years.
These results, like those in the First Report, appeared to indicate
that alcoholism can, indeed, be arrested and perhaps cured. But
the Second Report, too, came under strong attack, for example,
by John Wallace again:

'The Second Report was methodologically superior to the [First
Report]. However, when the results are examined for sustained non-problem drinking over time and are corrected for
invalid measurement of quantity/frequency [of drinking], the
best estimate of the sustained non-problem drinking rate is
around 3 percent to 4 percent. In short, at least 96 percent
of the Second Rand Report subjects failed to give evidence
of sustained non-problem drinking over the four-year follow-
up period. This is hardly an advertisement for the success
of controlled drinking in alcoholics.'

"In their efforts to discredit the disease concept, the proponents of controlled drinking resorted to some strange claims. For example, Stanton Peele, writing in *The Sciences,* said that the disease concept fosters irresponsibility, and provides an excuse for continued drinking.

"Anyone familiar with the modern treatment center would be excusably disturbed by this statement. John Wallace summed it up succinctly:

'At Edgehill-Newport, the disease model—including genetic, neurochemical, behavioral and cultural factors—is taught to patients to help them understand the etiology of their illness. Among the 12,000 or so patients we have treated, there has been no tendency for them to lean on the disease model in order to avoid irresponsibility for their actions. In fact, an accountability is stressed during treatment: a 'graduation medallion' given to each patient on completion of the program is inscribed: 'I am responsible.'

"A second strange claim by Peele in the same article in *The Sciences* was that people are put into treatment centers merely for getting drunk a few times after years of moderate drinking. Again Wallace remarked in response to Peele:

'In these days of stringent criteria for admission and continued stays (including extensive utilization reviews, third party payor, pre-certification of admissions, and rigorous managed-care patient audit), there is virtually no chance that a person would be admitted to treatment . . . in the absence of a significant prior history of drug or alcohol problems.'

"The efforts of the controlled drinking proponents are important only in that they mislead the alcoholic, and complicate the efforts of the treatment community. What the alcoholic who is resisting treament wants to hear more than anything else is that he or she *can* drink in a controlled fashion without paying the penalty of relapse and eventual death."[4]

We live in a relatively free society; diverse ideas flood the marketplace. In protection of my personal sobriety and life, I maintain this view: What has one lost if one chooses abstinence?

We need options in recovery. I hope that a wide variety of abstinence-based alternatives will emerge in time.

Q: What does "sobriety" mean to you personally?

A: I equate abstinence or sobriety with survival. *I am sober, therefore I am.* In sobriety I have whatever power I have. Without sobriety, I would be rendered powerless; the "I" of me, my "personhood" if you will, would be held captive in a bottle. I revel in my ongoing sobriety, in this "way of being." Empowered with the freedom to experience real life via sobriety, I now have the freedom to make choices. Some of my choices work and some don't. Existentialism in the raw? Perhaps.

Again, SOS is a freethought forum in recovery and I've expressed my own personal views here.

Q: I'd like to turn now to the administration and organization of SOS. How's the "home office" set up?

A: Our "home office," as you referred to it, has always served only as a clearinghouse. The SOS International Clearinghouse is presently located in Buffalo, New York, in the old quarters of CODESH (The Council for Democratic and Secular Humanism), a nonprofit educational organization and publisher of *Free Inquiry* magazine. Until June of 1990, the SOS Clearinghouse was located in my home in North Hollywood, California. CODESH had agreed to fund SOS Clearinghouse activities, publishing and mailing out the SOS newsletter, *Save Our Selves,* to our rapidly growing readership, nationally and abroad.

There were no salaried personnel at the clearinghouse then; the North Hollywood clearinghouse relied entirely on volunteers. SOS grew very quickly, so I "shuffled off to Buffalo," where I accepted a position at CODESH. SOS has applied for separate incorporation as a nonprofit educational organization.

At the present time we're still loosely affiliated with CODESH, but CODESH has never set policy for SOS. We plan to continue a loose affiliation with CODESH; after all, secular humanists are about as secular as one can get. Many SOS members, being secular persons, have an interest in the CODESH organization, but many more SOS members have little or no interest in CODESH. We're comfortable with that as a separate issue. The SOS mission is *recovery* via free, autonomous grass-roots self-help support groups, not secular humanism.

SOS is still "in the red" financially, and CODESH continues to help keep the clearinghouse afloat. The only means of income for SOS is through subscriptions to its newsletter, through voluntary contributions from its grass-roots membership-at-large, and by the sale of recovery materials (books, tapes, brochures) through the clearinghouse. The goal of the SOS International Clearinghouse is eventually to pay back in full the money advanced to us from CODESH and to become self-supporting.

The SOS International Clearinghouse does *not* dictate policy to the more than 1,000 free, autonomous grass-roots SOS self-help support groups. Each SOS group determines its needs among its local membership.

Q: What happens to SOS members? Do they have to attend SOS for the rest of their lives? What happens in the SOS version of recovery?

A: As an abstinence movement, SOS offers a freethought forum providing an informal support system for recovery. All persons grow at their own pace. SOS members share in confidence with each other their separate-issue life challenges. Some folks initially attend some SOS meetings and then choose to attend no longer, preferring a "private recovery," if you will. Research has shown that many persons achieve a "clean and sober" lifestyle without support of any kind. Their recovery, as is the recovery of those in AA, Women for Sobriety, etc., is as valid as anyone else's recovery.

SOS members tend to view SOS meetings as an awareness tool. Most do not "play out their lives" in daily meetings of any kind. Since we credit ourselves for our achievement and maintenance of sobriety, most of us utilize the "citizens of the world" concept, i.e., we get on with our lives as clean and sober alcoholics/addicts, while continuing to take full advantage of SOS group support and to feel good from altruistically giving back support to those new to recovery. Although some persons get sober and sit on the bleachers of life, scarfing down donuts and gallons of caffeinated coffee laced with refined sugar, chain-smoking cigarettes, and being generally complacent—except about the individual sobriety priority—many others opt for the engagé position, at least to some extent. Arsenio Hall, a popular television talk show host, might say that "We get busy!"

There's lots going on in life beyond drinking and drugging!

Q: Regarding "sober alcoholics" on medication—what's the SOS policy?

A: The vast majority of members in any abstinence group interpret recovery as being "clean and sober." However, some alcoholics and addicts also suffer from what treatment professionals call "dual diagnosis." They may be manic-depressive or schizophrenic, requiring medications *responsibly* prescribed by physicians to treat their physiological chemical imbalance. This is a medical matter, not an SOS "policy" matter, and not always subject to easy answers or black-and-white solutions. Certainly there's a difference between those formerly hooked on various addictive medications who choose to become and stay "clean and sober" and those members who seem to require *responsibly* prescribed medications. Members of any abstinence group including SOS choose abstinence. Medical problems are dealt with as a separate issue.

Q: How have chemical dependency treatment professionals, referral agencies, and the courts viewed the advent of SOS?

A: Since 1987, Los Angeles courts have given persons mandated to attend abstinence support groups a choice between AA and SOS. As they've learned about SOS, many other courts across the country have followed suit, pleased to have an additional option. Thousands of members of the helping professions—physicians, psychologists, psychiatrists, professional counselors, nurses, chemical dependency treatment professionals, as well as related referral agencies—have happily utilized SOS groups as a viable recovery alternative for their patients and clients. The climate is changing in the recovery field.

Having said this, I'd like to relate incidents in which SOS has experienced resistance from "12-steppers." On various occasions AA central-office volunteers have told persons seeking options in recovery:

"I don't know how you can reach the SOS Clearinghouse, and if I did I wouldn't tell you."

"AA saved my life! It's the only program that works! This other outfit, a bunch of atheists, holds meetings for 'dry drunks.' When they leave God out of it, they're not 'sober' in my book!"

Other AA hotline workers, however, have reportedly said, "AA is for anyone who wants it. If you'd like another option in recovery, go for it! Whatever works!"

Treatment center professionals have been both mean-spirited and open-minded. A recent incident is indeed heartening and has been repeated in treatment facilities nationwide. The program director of a major treatment center in New York State, familiar with SOS and open to options in recovery, invited a local SOS group to hold meetings in the treatment facility on an open basis (both patients and outsiders in recovery were welcome). At first, this action was met with objections from 12-stepping treatment personnel. As time passed and patients in sufficient numbers who had not been comfortable with AA responded dramatically to treatment, the same 12-step adherents came to the program director, apologizing and acknowledging that without the SOS option a significant number of patients would not have had an effective recovery experience in treatment.

Recently, an extremely distraught psychologist, in practice for many years, called the SOS Clearinghouse conveying that his daughter and son were hooked on drugs. He said that he realized alcoholism and other drug addictions had to be approached as the priority and as a separate issue, not as a psychological "symptom." Both siblings had almost died; they had not fared well with the AA approach. SOS assisted him in finding a treatment center that was open to options. This sort of thing happens all too frequently, but change is here.

Schick Shadel Hospitals, for example, offer medical synchrotherapy (aversion treatment), AA, and also other options, respecting personal philosophies both in treatment and in aftercare. Unfortunately, Schick Hospitals are only available in three states: California, Texas, and Washington. Heretofore, AA was pushed as the only way to recovery in virtually all inpatient and outpatient treatment facilities. Certified alcoholism counselors (often 12-step zealots) told their charges: "If you don't accept the AA philosophy, you will die out there." This is obviously not true, and these attitudes have to some extent mercifully changed.

SOS is not in competition with any group. In offering *a* way, and a freethought forum approach, we're positively thrilled with folks finding recovery—any recovery—however it's achieved!

Q: I know you're not a guru and that SOS offers a "leaderless" approach. How do new persons respond to you and to SOS?

A: Appropriately, I'm happy to say! Newcomers and long-term sobrietists, pleased to find an option, have expressed reasonable appreciation. As "just plain Jim" (warts and all), I've felt no tugs at the "hem of my garment." AA has an "official" brochure, albeit an old one, still readily available through its World Publishing Services, titled *Why We Were **Chosen*** (emphasis mine). Some AA members openly state that they believe the book *Alcoholics Anonymous* (the "Big Book") to be divinely inspired.

What is our structure? What do we offer the newcomer when we have no 12 "spiritual" steps, no "guru" sponsors, no necessity to believe in a "higher power" to achieve and to maintain sobriety? We offer what other secular self-help groups offer: *support* from those who know what you're talking about and feeling from their own personal experiences. We offer *empathy* and *compassion.* We offer a variety of recovery "tools": printed materials, audio and visual tapes. We offer *ourselves,* demonstrating live and in color that sobriety can be happily achieved and maintained by secular as well as religious persons in a secular support setting. We offer *mutual respect,* focusing on "doing sobriety," not on telling each other how to live, deliberately not offering a step program or "design for living." We offer *encouragement,* and we credit ourselves individually and each other for achievement and maintenance of sobriety. We are egalitarian in approach, not elitist. We *share* our thoughts and feelings without a rigid meeting structure, allowing for a more relaxed recovery process.

Prior to achieving sobriety newcomers are usually chemically detoxed professionally within a protected environment before attending any self-help support group. We are *not* a treatment facility (and neither is AA). Treatment facilities consider us an "aftercare" option (as is AA). Our approach to achieving and maintaining sobriety encourages newcomers to draw from whatever sources they find valuable in creating their own design for living—structured or free-form—thus respecting diversity.

Persons new to recovery in any program will initially feel discomfort. We simply try to be there for each other. I'd like to add that new persons who have had minimal (or no) exposure to the AA experience (and those who've attended SOS after having achieved sobriety—perhaps many years of sobriety—on their own) seem to express less fear and discomfort. Why? New people without the AA experience have no AA admonitions, no "struck drunk" trepidations to contend with. Long-term on-their-own sobrietists have already experienced themselves sober for a number of years without AA dogma but are happy to find secular support groups that they had wanted "way back when."

We feel this quote describes our support and structure and our egalitarian freethought forum viewpoint nicely:

> Don't walk in front of me
> I may not follow
> Don't walk behind me
> I may not lead
> Walk beside me
> And just be my friend
> —Albert Camus

Q: What are your personal hopes for SOS in the future? How do you think "recovery methods" and related research will evolve to address rampant global alcohol-and drug-addiction problems?

A: I hope SOS will thrive as a friendly alternative, one of many abstinence-based approaches that, I hope, will emerge in the not-too-distant future.

Although my personal sobriety is not dependent on the continuing existence of SOS—and that's the general viewpoint of SOS members regarding dependency on any group—SOS fills a need, as evidenced by its rapid growth in the five years of its existence. I hope AA and other 12-step abstinence groups will continue to flourish, and that AA will eventually update its precepts while still honoring its roots and those very dedicated pioneers who originated it.

We already see evidence that research validates the SOS "separate-issue" approach. We human beings are chemical creatures. We'll know much more in ten or twenty years, but, for now, we can work together as allies in recovery and research, utilizing the scientific method as well as compassion in that process.

One more thing: Another avenue that should be taken is *prevention through education.* It's worked well with tobacco addiction, and I think it's time to scrutinize the alcoholic beverage industry as well, as John Lanagan does later in this book.

Notes

1. *Alcoholics Anonymous* (New York: Alcoholics Anonymous World Services, 1976), pp. 59–60.

2. James Christopher, *Unhooked: Staying Sober and Drug Free* (Buffalo, N.Y.: Prometheus Books, 1989), pp. 51–54.

3. Jeffrey Moussaieff Masson, *Against Therapy: Emotional Tyranny and the Myth of Psychological Healing* (New York: Atheneum/Macmillan Publishing Co., 1988), Preface, xv.

4. Kenneth Blum, Ph.D., in collaboration with James E. Payne, *Alcohol and the Addictive Brain* (New York: The Free Press/Macmillan Publishing Co., 1991), pp. 237–47.

2. Recovery Experiences of SOS Members: Preliminary Findings

William M. London, Karen E. Courchaine,
and David L. Yoho

Abstract

Thirty members of Secular Organizations for Sobriety (SOS) from across the United States returned questionnaires on demographics and recovery experiences. All respondents were white adults, and most were college-educated nontheists with a history of chronic alcohol-related problems. Respondents had attended SOS a mean of 4.8 months, and during that time only six members reported using any drug other than tobacco. Most of those who attended a 12-step group or other treatment program reported being told that it would be impossible to stay sober without turning their lives over to a "higher power." Only respondents who were told this rated treatment or 12-step groups as harmful. Most respondents rated SOS as helpful and none rated it harmful. Consequently, SOS appears to be a viable alternative for recovery for at least some addicted individuals.

*   *   *

The establishment of safe, effective methods for the promotion of recovery from addiction requires controlled, long-term, prospective (i.e., starting before addicted subjects enter treatment) evaluation studies using valid, reliable outcome measures applied to clearly defined populations. Yet, in the more than fifty years of accumulated literature on Alcoholics Anonymous and other 12-step groups, there is a notable absence of scientific evidence from well-designed outcome evaluation studies.

Twelve-step groups have been popularly acclaimed for promoting recovery primarily on the basis of large numbers of anecdotal reports of personal success stories. Although membership survey data published in the newsletter *A.A. Grapevine* quantify success stories, the data are still only anecdotal because they don't describe (1) how well survey respondents represent any definable population of AA members; (2) what percentage of those individuals who initially try 12-step meetings winds up worse off then they were before attending meetings; and (3) what percentage winds up improving. Moreover, the experiences of AA members do not represent the experiences of addicts who learn to maintain sobriety without joining any type of fellowship (Stall and Biernacki, 1986).

Although anecdotal data provide no conclusive support for the safety and efficacy of AA, such data suggest that some addicts may benefit (or be harmed) and how they do so. Any claims made that the 12-step method is the "best," the "only," or a "highly efficacious" path to addiction recovery are not supported by data. Yet it is not unusual for treatment professionals in the U.S. to offer the 12-step model to clients as the *only* recommended path to recovery.

This chapter describes the first attempt to quantify SOS "success stories" by surveying members on their experiences with SOS and with traditional approaches to recovery. The findings are no less anecdotal than most data on AA. *Thus, in no way do the findings of this study provide definitive support for any one approach to recovery over any other.* However, like other anecdotal reports on self-help experiences, the study identifies possibilities to be examined by treatment professionals, addiction researchers, and addicts motivated toward recovery.

Method

One hundred copies of a questionnaire constructed by the authors and with a letter describing the rights of human subjects regarding informed consent were distributed for voluntary participation of SOS members at (1) an SOS meeting in Buffalo, New York, by the first author; (2) an SOS meeting in Southgate, Michigan, by the convenor of the meeting; and (3) the first National SOS Conference in California by the recognized SOS national leader, James Christopher. Respondents in Michigan and California were instructed to mail the completed questionnaires to the first author. Data were collected in 1988 and 1989.

Questions addressed personal background; history of substance abuse; and recovery experiences, perspectives, and progress. Respondents were given the opportunity to write explanations of any of their responses.

Results

Demographics

A total of 30 completed questionnaires were returned. The sample consisted of 9 female and 21 male whites from western (18), eastern (6), and midwestern (6) states. Nearly half the respondents (14) were from California, where the first SOS conference was held.

The mean age of respondents was 50.1 years with a range of 32 to 71 years. Fourteen were married and eight were divorced or separated. Of the 24 who had college degrees, 9 had master's degrees and 3, doctorates. Occupations varied considerably, with the most frequent response being "retired" (6) followed by "counselor" (4). There were 21 nontheists and 5 who reported a religion other than a mainline Christian denomination (e.g., Unitarian). However, before age 18, seven of the respondents had been Catholic and 12 others had identified their primary religion as a recognizable Protestant faith.

Treatment History

The mean number of SOS meetings attended was 17.0, with a range from one to forty meetings. The mean number of months since respondents first attended was 4.8, with a range from less than one month to fifteen months. Twenty-five respondents reported their last attendance at an SOS meeting to be from less than one month to no more than four months before the completion of the questionnaire.

Most of the respondents reported a history of professional treatment for addiction (Table 1). Twelve (47.0 percent) responded "yes" to the question: "Did a treatment professional ever tell you that it would be impossible for you to stay sober unless you turned your life over to a higher power?" Of the eighteen respondents who reported receiving professional treatment, twelve answered "yes" to this question.

Table 1
Treatment History

	Number of Respondents Out of 30
Received professional treatment	18
Received professional aftercare or outpatient treatment	15
Currently receiving aftercare or outpatient treatment	3
Ever received professional detoxification	9
Ever received inpatient care	13

All but one respondent reported a history of attendance at 12-step meetings. Twenty-eight indicated attendance at Alcoholics Anonymous meetings (Table 2). Almost 76 percent (or twenty-two of those who attended a 12-step meeting) answered "yes" to the question: "Did a member of a spiritually oriented 12-step meeting ever tell you that it would be impossible for you to stay sober unless you turned your life over to a higher power?"

Table 2
Experience with 12-Step Groups

	Number Out of 30 Who Attended	Median Estimated Meetings Attended
Any 12-step meeting	29	—
Alcoholics Anonymous	28	130
Alanon	4	15
Codependents	3	8
Adult Children of Alcoholics	3	6
Unspecified 12-step group	1	—

Figure 1 summarizes ratings of respondents' experiences with outpatient treatment/aftercare, inpatient treatment, 12-step groups, and SOS. Most of the respondents who received professional treatment rated the overall effect of the treatment as somewhat or very helpful in supporting the maintenance of their sobriety. Less than half (twelve) gave 12-step meetings an overall effect rating of somewhat or very helpful on this question. More than half (sixteen) rated the overall effect of SOS as very helpful, and nine rated the overall effect of SOS as somewhat helpful in supporting the maintenance of their sobriety. Six of the nine female respondents rated SOS as very helpful, and two rated it somewhat helpful.

Figure 1. Subjective Ratings of Recovery Programs
in Supporting the Maintenance of Sobriety

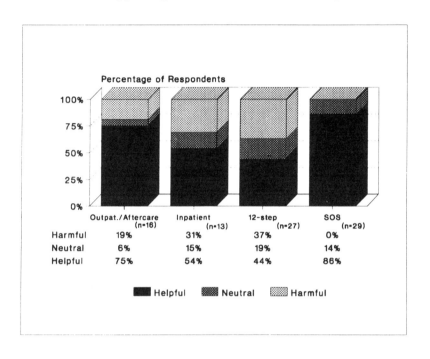

None of the respondents rated the overall effect of SOS as harmful. However, ratings of somewhat or very harmful were given by two of the fifteen respondents who provided ratings of their outpatient treatment/aftercare experience, four of thirteen who provided ratings of their inpatient treatment experience, and ten of twenty-seven who provided ratings of their experience with 12-step meetings.

Two of the ten in outpatient treatment/aftercare who were told by a professional that it would be "impossible to stay sober unless they turned their lives over to a higher power" rated the treatment as somewhat or very harmful. None of the five respondents who were not told this rated their outpatient/aftercare experience as harmful. This relationship between what treatment providers told respondents about the need for a higher power and how respondents rated outpatient/aftercare was not found to be statistically significant.

Three of the ten receiving inpatient treatment who were told by a treatment professional that it would be "impossible to stay sober unless they turned their lives over to a higher power" rated the overall effect of their treatment as somewhat or very harmful. Neither of the two respondents not told this rated their inpatient treatment as harmful. However, this relationship was not found to be statistically significant for inpatients.

Ten of the twenty who reported that a member told them that it would be "impossible to stay sober unless they turned their lives over to a higher power" rated the overall effect of the 12-step meetings as somewhat or very harmful. Of the seven respondents who were not told this, none rated the overall effect of the meetings as harmful. The relationship between what respondents were told about the need for a higher power at 12-step meetings and their ratings of the meetings *was* statistically significant.*

Recovery History

Table 3 reports the number of respondents who reported a history of chronic problems (of a mental, physical, emotional, or social nature) with various drugs, and their progress since beginning SOS attendance. Although almost every respondent reported a history of problems with alcohol, and twelve reported problems with tobacco, few respondents reported a history of problems with other drugs. Six of the thirty respondents reported using alcohol and/or drugs other than tobacco since attending SOS and two of the six reported use that they claimed resulted in no problems. Re-

---

*Chi-square = 5.6, d.f. = 1, n = 27, p < .05. This statistical significance means such a relationship would be expected to result by chance fewer than 5 times if this study were repeated 100 times with other samples of SOS members.

Table 3
History of Chronic Problems with Drugs and
Use/Problematic Use Since Attending SOS

Drug	Number Who Ever Experienced Chronic Problems (%)		Number Who Used at Least Once Since Attending SOS (%)	Number Who Used Problematically at Least Once Since Attending SOS (%)
Alcohol	29	(97)	4 (13)	3 (10)
Tobacco	12*	(40)	7 (23)**	2 (7)
Marijuana	8	(27)	2 (7)	2 (7)
Sedatives	4	(13)	2 (7)	1 (3)
Opiates	3	(10)	1 (3)	1 (3)
Amphetamines	2	(7)	0 (0)	0 (0)
Cocaine	2	(7)	0 (0)	0 (0)
LSD	2	(7)	0 (0)	0 (0)
Any Drug Other Than Tobacco	30	(100)	6 (20)	4 (13)
Any Drug	30	(100)	11 (37)	7 (23)

*Eighteen or 60% admitted to being smokers although they did not admit to having chronic problems of a mental, physical, emotional, or social nature associated with tobacco.

**Each of these respondents reported daily use, yet only two described their use as problematic.

spondents reported being drug-free for a mean of 31.8 months, with a median of 16.5 months. Thirteen respondents reported being drug-free for more than twenty-four months. The longest reported period of abstention by a respondent was 168 months (fourteen years).

Comments of Respondents

Participants were given the opportunity to elaborate or to clarify their responses to items in the questionnaire. Several respondents commented about judgmental members and dogma they encountered in AA meetings. Two addressed the higher-power dogmas in AA. One was a 34-year-old female who had attended an estimated forty SOS meetings over a nine-month period during which she abstained completely from drugs other than tobacco. She rated the overall effect of SOS in supporting the maintenance of her sobriety as very helpful, but she rated AA as somewhat harmful.

> I quit drugs cold turkey September 4, 1987 (after chronic use for 18 years). I attended AA regularly for 6 months, but I was very depressed as I don't believe in God, and I think the higher power stuff is unrealistic. Since I found SOS, I am no longer depressed and I am able to stay sober with the support and comfort of others who have the same non-beliefs as I do.

A 54-year-old male who had attended an estimated twelve SOS meetings over a four-month period rated the overall effect of both SOS and AA as very helpful in supporting the maintenance of his sobriety. Yet he noted: "I was and am a one stepper since the beginning of my involvement with AA (5 years). I did not feel good about myself or sobriety until SOS." (A "one stepper" is one who doesn't go beyond admitting one's powerlessness over alcohol to move on to step 2, which requires that one give one's will over to that of a "higher power.")

Apparently AA helped this respondent to maintain sobriety, while SOS helped him feel better about maintaining it. However, it appears that he didn't leave AA because of its dogma on a "higher power," but over encountering another traditional attitude in AA. He explained: "I was the secretary of a beginner's AA group and had to quit because of problems caused by older AA members for new members that were dual-addicted."

Traditionally, AA has limited itself to helping alcoholics to abstain from alcohol, and not to helping dually addicted alcoholics to abstain from other drugs (who can be helped in various other 12-step groups modeled after AA). Yet, AA also warns its members to avoid using other addictive drugs. This warning may be prudent, in general, but it may cause problems as inflexible dogma, especially when it conflicts with equally prudent medical advice. A 48-year-old female respondent who was completing her ninth uninterrupted year of sobriety and who had needed prescribed medication for a back problem describes how

> in the past, I believe prescribed use of pain medication, without recovery group support, led [me] back to alcohol, and subsequent abuse [in the 1970s] for me. The AA where I "grew up," in San Jose, California, frowned upon any and all pain- or mood-altering medication. I have since seen members manage these successfully for short periods with support from fellow members. Disclosure and refusal to call such disclosed, medically prescribed use a "slip," seem to have reduced the hiding and group alienation that I as well as others had experienced.

Despite the possibility that support for short periods of medically necessary chemical pain management might be available from AA, this woman noted that she would seek such support from SOS (which she rated "very helpful" after attending twenty to twenty-five meetings in four months) if she again required pain medication. Her preference for SOS appears to be due to the harmful, dogmatic aspects she noted in attending hundreds of AA meetings:

- *Moralistic* terms applied even where denied.
- Duality of "good/bad" played into shame came well into sobriety.
- Continuing emotional self-abuse (judgmentalism, rather than focus on what *works*).

- Patriarchical deistic language.
- Abusive sponsorship because of above limitations plus co-dependency issues.
- Loss of autonomy and self-empowerment; infantilization; cognitive and discriminative shut-down due to "don't think" messages (rely directly on suggestion/directives—i.e., "utilize, don't analyze"—beyond stages where direction-taking was appropriate).

A 36-year-old female respondent who had attended an estimated thirty SOS meetings over a six-month period expressed a similar sentiment about AA dogma: "Compared to AA, SOS offers me a wider range of humanity—by that I mean, in a current space of lapses, I don't feel the 'judgment of soul' as I did with AA."

This respondent rated the overall effect of SOS on her as somewhat helpful and the overall effect of 12-step meetings on her as somewhat harmful. She noted three occasions of problematic alcohol use since attending SOS but suggested, "I *do* feel the need for more meetings, which I feel would facilitate my getting more of a handle on my lapses."

Two respondents identified very helpful AA groups with the same unique characteristic. One, a 59-year-old female, continually drug-free for two months since attending her first of ten SOS meetings, explained: "I am also attending a weekly AA meeting (since 9/88) named We Agnostics, which I find to be as helpful as SOS."

A 63-year-old male, drug-free for two months since attending the first of his fourteen SOS meetings, elaborated further:

I first attended AA meetings in England in 1957 and stayed sober for approximately fourteen years. I had difficulty with the spiritual aspects of AA, but the support I received helped me to stay sober. I "slipped" shortly after entering psychoanalysis and eventually had to be hospitalized. For the next several years I was a serious periodic drinker, requiring hospitalization on many occasions. During this time, however, I was sober for seven years, and for up to three years on several occasions, all without attending any support groups but relying on psychiatric help. The last time I drank, during 9/88, I again required hospitalization, and by this time had given up on both therapy and AA. But I discovered an AA meeting for agnostics and SOS. Both have been extremely helpful.

Others also noted that the support provided by AA (and not just agnostic groups within AA) is helpful. The 48-year-old female respondent with recurring back problems described the following aspects of AA as "very helpful": "emergence from isolation, identification of common problems with others, sense of acceptance, and disease concept."

Similarly, a 34-year-old male, sober for almost eight years, who attended SOS about twenty times over a ten-month period explained: "AA was a tremendous help socially, offering me essential support outside meetings. The meetings *per se* I found worthless after the first few weeks." Having been able to stay sober for about seven years without SOS, he rated SOS "somewhat helpful" in its overall effect on his maintaining abstinence.

Another respondent who rated SOS "somewhat helpful" also had an extended period of sobriety before SOS. The respondent, a 51-year-old male who attended thirty-three SOS meetings in seven months, commented:

> Regarding use of mood-altering substances, I stopped using these prior to my affiliation with SOS (over three years prior). However I do not wish to minimize the contribution of SOS to my sobriety and emotional balance.

Discussion

Although countless addicted individuals have successfully maintained abstinence through participation in 12-step recovery groups such as AA, countless other addicts find such groups to be unappealing

(Ogborne and Glaser, 1981; Saxe, Dougherty, Esty, and Fine, 1983; Tournier, 1979). Not surprisingly, our SOS respondents tended to find the religious and dogmatic character of AA to be unappealing.

Although AA members often describe the groups as "spiritual" and endorsing no particular religious view, AA has its roots in the Oxford Group Movement, which was originally known as the First Century Christian Fellowship (Orford, 1986). Its style has been compared to "the Protestant revival meeting, where the sinner seeks salvation through personal testimony, by public contrition and submission to a higher power" (Peele, 1985, p. 31). Six of AA's suggested 12 steps to Recovery mention either "Power greater than ourselves," "God," or "Him." Step 11 calls for seeking conscious contact with God through prayer. The Lord's Prayer and the Serenity Prayer, which are commonly recited at 12-Step meetings, are recognizably Christian and thus reflect more than just a nonsectarian "spiritual" search.

Acceptance of and submission to a higher power can undoubtedly aid certain individuals in recovery from addiction, but our data suggest that this can be counterproductive when presented as a requirement for recovery. The only respondents who rated 12-Step groups and professional treatment programs harmful were offered this orthodox AA perspective. Despite distributing pamphlets ostensibly designed to reach out to alcoholic atheists and agnostics, AA's "Big Book" rejects the possibility of nontheistic recovery without a "spiritual experience":

> To one who feels he is an atheist or agnostic such an experience seems impossible, but to continue as he is means disaster, especially if he is an alcoholic of the hopeless variety. To be doomed to an alcoholic death or to live on a spiritual basis are not always easy alternatives to face. (*Alcoholics Anonymous,* 1976, p. 44)

The AA groups for agnostics attended by two of our respondents apparently did not go strictly by the book.

The typical successful AA participant has been characterized by religiosity, conformity, authoritarianism, and lower education (Miller and Hester, 1986). One need not fit this description to benefit from AA, but many who do not (e.g., our SOS respondents) may reject AA meetings. If such individuals are offered no alternative, they may indeed come to see themselves as "alcoholics of the hopeless variety" and avoid personal efforts at recovery. Thus, in some cases, referrals to AA can be counterproductive.

It is possible that referrals to SOS might, in some cases, also be counterproductive. Those who fit the profile of the typical successful AA member might feel uncomfortable in the atmosphere of free inquiry fostered by SOS. Future studies will need to examine how appealing SOS participation is for adolescents, young adults, nonwhites, polydrug abusers, those with little formal schooling, and other groups not represented in our sample.

Our findings indicate that some alcoholics can maintain abstinence for at least several months while attending SOS. While the data do not provide any conclusive evidence in support of the effectiveness of SOS, most respondents indicated that they believed SOS helped them to remain sober or at least to enjoy a sober lifestyle more completely.

This preliminary study was limited by its low response rate and small convenience sample, which cannot be viewed as representative of all SOS members. Those who completed and returned the questionnaires were likely to be particularly enthusiastic members (as are AA members who respond to its surveys), especially those respondents who attend the SOS conference. Larger surveys of representative samples of members of all SOS groups known by the SOS Clearinghouse are needed.

References

Alcoholics Anonymous, 3d ed. (New York: Alcoholics Anonymous World Services, 1976).

W. R. Miller and R. K. Hester, "The Effectiveness of Alcoholism Treatment: What Research Reveals," in *Treating Addictive Behaviors*, ed. W. R. Miller and N. Heather (New York: Plenum Press, 1986).

A. C. Ogborne, and F. B. Glaser, "Characteristics of Affiliates of Alcoholics Anonymous: A Review of the Literature," *Journal of Studies on Alcohol* 42 (1981): 661–75.

J. Orford, "Critical Conditions for Change in the Addictive Behaviors," in *Treating Addictive Behaviors*, ed. W. R. Miller and N. Heather (New York: Plenum Press, 1986).

S. Peele, *The Meaning of Addiction* (Lexington, Mass.: Lexington, 1985).

L. Saxe, D. Doughtery, K. Esty, and M. Fine, *The Effectiveness and Costs of Alcoholism Treatment* (Washington, D.C.: Office of Technology Assessment, 1983).

R. Stall and P. Biernacki, "Spontaneous Remission from the Problematic Use of Substances: An Inductive Model Derived from a Comparative Analysis of the Alcohol, Opiate, Tobacco, and Food/Obesity Literatures," *The International Journal of the Addictions* 21 (1986): 1–23.

R. E. Tournier, "Alcoholics Anonymous as Treatment and as Ideology." *Journal of Studies on Alcohol* 40 (1979): 230–39.

Acknowledgments

The authors wish to acknowledge the assistance of James Christopher and Thelma Murrell in collecting data, and Jim Jones in analyzing the data.

3. SOS Membership Survey: Preliminary Results

Gerard J. Connors, Kurt H. Dermen, and Mark Duerr

Packets of questionnaires were mailed to 200 individuals on the SOS convenor mailing list. These individuals were randomly selected from the list according to geographic region. Regions were represented proportionately (i.e., if 30% of the entire list was from the Northwest, then 30% of the sample was selected from the Northwest). These packets each included twenty questionnaires with instructions for the convenors to distribute them at their next meetings, to tell their group members to fill out the questionnaires after the meeting and mail them in the enclosed return envelope, and to fill out a questionnaire plus a "convenor form" themselves. A total of 4,000 questionnaires (200 packets of 20 questionnaires each) were mailed. Of these 161 scorable questionnaires were returned; those from individuals who had never been to an SOS meeting or who did not attend SOS for alcohol-related purposes were not included. Questionnaires were returned from twenty-two different states, with California, Florida, New

York, and Massachusetts each accounting for 10% or more of the respondents.

The sample was almost entirely white (99.4%), and three-quarters were male (73.4%). The average age of the sample was 47.09 years, with a range of 24–72 years. A majority of respondents (58.9%) were unmarried. Of the remainder, 27.2% were divorced, 26.6% had never been married, 3.2% were separated, and 1.3% were widows or widowers. This sample was highly educated, reporting an average of 16.45 years of schooling. All had received at least a high school diploma and 79.5% received some form of college degree (13.5% had an associate's degree, 34.6% a bachelor's degree, 16.7% a master's degree, and 14.7% had earned a doctorate). The average individual income was $31,000. Approximately half of the sample worked full time (52.6%). The rest were retired (12.8%), worked part time (9.6%), were not employed (3.8%), were disabled (3.2%), or checked "other" (9.6%). Most of those who checked "other" were self-employed (57.1%). Most respondents (83.5%) had some form of religious upbringing, primarily Protestant (44.3%) or Catholic (27.8%), before their eighteenth birthday. The most common Protestant denominations cited were Presbyterian (25.8%), Methodist (18.2%), Episcopalian (12.1%), and Baptist (10.6%). A large proportion of SOS respondents (70.3%) reported no current religious affiliation. Most described themselves as either atheist (36.9%) or agnostic (33.1%). For those who did report a religious affiliation, (sixteen individuals), the most commonly named was Unitarian. Most of the sample were not church attenders. Only 5.1% reported that they were religious and attended church; the average number of times these individuals attended church in the last year was 5.82.

Most individuals learned about SOS from either the news media (34.8%) or from an SOS member (21.3%). The majority were attending because of concerns over their alcohol (75.8%) or drug use (5.1%), and almost all (95.5%) had attended more than one meeting. Only 29.5% were simultaneously attending Alcoholics Anonymous (AA) meetings. The average number of SOS meetings attended during the last year was 29.02, with 3.89 attendances occurring during the last month. The total number of SOS meetings ever attended averaged 45.37 meetings. The average attendance at the last SOS meeting was 7.68 (with a range of 2–20 individuals), and the meeting lasted an hour and a quarter. For most SOS members, there are only one (48.1%) or two (28.6%) meetings available per week. For about half the members (53.6%), this is sufficient; the rest would like more meetings to be available. Almost all respondents attend SOS on a voluntary basis (98.7%), and 85.1% plan long-term attendance (9.1% plan short-term attendance). Abstinence is the goal for most (85.5%). Finally, the majority of respondents (85%) find attending SOS to be helpful in maintaining their sobriety, with 52% finding it very helpful and another 33% finding it somewhat helpful.

Almost all respondents (95.5%) had attended at least one AA meeting, with over half having attended over 100 meetings. The average recent AA attendance over the last year was 56.44 meetings, and over the last month the average was 4.5 meetings. AA meetings are much more available than are SOS meetings, with 16.5% of the respondents reporting over 100 meetings available per week and another 24.7% simply writing in "lots," "unlimited," or "millions." However, this is irrelevant to the majority of respondents, as 61.3% do not plan to attend AA in the future (28.9% still plan long-term AA attendance and 6.3% plan short-term attendance). The average AA meeting was reported to include thirty-seven people and to last sixty-nine minutes. Just over half of the sample found AA to be helpful in maintaining sobriety (26.5% found it very helpful and 29.3% found it somewhat helpful). However, 23.1% found AA to be neither helpful nor harmful and 19% found it to be harmful (9.5% somewhat harmful and 9.5% very harmful).

Most SOS members report that they are currently abstinent (70%) or mostly abstinent (16%). Those who are abstinent have been so for an average of 6.3 years. The average SOS member first took a drink at 14.5 years of age, first became drunk at 17, and first developed a drinking problem at 29. The alcohol problem typically lasted for around fourteen years. When drinking, 42.1% were steady drinkers, 26.3% were periodic or binge drinkers, and 27% followed both patterns. Many symptoms were reported as a consequence of drinking, with the most common being hangovers (92.4%), nausea/vomiting (86.7%), loss of control (79.7%), blackouts (77.8%), and vague feelings of fear and anxiety (77.2%). Less common but still reported were severe shakes (40.5%), hallucinations (25.9%), delirium tremens (13.3%), and seizures or convulsions (7%). The most frequently reported problems caused by alcohol use were psychological (an average of 6.56 on a scale from 1–10) and social/ interpersonal (6.2 on the scale). However, alcohol was also at least moderately problematic in several other areas, including (in descending order) family, sleep, physical health, marriage, work, and finances. Less frequently reported were sexual, drug-abuse, and legal problems associated with drinking. The sample has utilized a variety of treatment modalities for alcohol problems. Almost half have seen a private therapist (49.3%), 41.6% have been in inpatient treatment, 38.6% have been in outpatient treatment, 29% have seen a private doctor, 26% have been in detoxification, and 23.9% have taken part in marriage/family counseling.

Two-thirds (68.2%) of the SOS respondents report having used drugs other than alcohol or prescription medications at some point in their lives, and over half (55.3%) have experienced drug-related problems or dependence. Those individuals who have never used drugs were not included in the following percentages. Almost all members are currently abstinent (87.6%) or mostly abstinent (10.6%) and have been for an average of 7.7 years. The typical member first used drugs at age 20 and first got high at the same age. The most commonly abused drugs were marijuana (37.9%), sedatives/ tranquilizers (24.3%), and amphetamines/stimulants (21.4%). Also abused were hallucinogens (19.3%) and cocaine/crack (15.7%). Drug abuse did not cause as many problems in this sample as alcohol abuse: only psychological problems (an average of 4.15 on a scale of 1–10), alcohol problems (3.52), and social/interpersonal problems

(3.24) were reported in the moderate range. The most common treatment approaches utilized by this sample for their drug problems were a private therapist (22%), Narcotics Anonymous (21%), and inpatient treatment (11%). Finally, 42% of the entire sample were smokers.

The Experience

4. Welcome to SOS!

The SOS meeting depicted in this chapter follows the standard format currently in use at SOS gatherings throughout the country. The participants in the meeting are based on actual people; the experiences and feelings they relate are *true* and drawn from minimally edited, taped interviews. Only the comments made by Sam in the role of convenor were especially written for this chapter; the personal testimonies of Sam and all other group members are *real.*

*   *   *

Sam: Welcome to SOS. My name is Sam, I'm a sober alcoholic, and I've been asked to moderate tonight's meeting.

Secular Organizations for Sobriety/Save Our Selves is dedicated to providing a path to sobriety that is an alternative to those paths depending upon supernatural beliefs. We respect diversity, welcome healthy skepticism, encourage rational thinking as well as the expression of our feelings, and we each take responsibility for our individual sobriety daily.

This is a sobriety meeting. Our focus is on the priority of abstaining from alcohol and other mind-altering drugs.

We respect the anonymity of each person in this room. This

is a self-help, nonprofessional group. At this meeting we share our experiences, understandings, thoughts, and feelings.

Various pieces of SOS literature are available on the table in the corner for anyone who would like some. I've also posted a schedule of SOS and Families-and-Friends group meetings on the corkboard in the rear. Please check these out for activities that might interest you.

Does anyone have any announcements?

We celebrate various lengths of sobriety in these meetings. Is there anyone here who has under thirty days of continuous sobriety? Sixty days . . . ninety days . . . six months . . . nine months? Is anyone celebrating a yearly anniversary tonight? If you have an anniversary date coming up, please let me know after the meeting, and we'll prepare a celebration for that date.

Tonight, I have asked Louise to read the suggested Guidelines for Sobriety.

Louise: To break the cycle of denial and achieve sobriety, we first acknowledge that we are alcoholics/addicts:

- We reaffirm this truth daily and accept without reservation—one day at a time—the fact that as clean and sober individuals, we cannot and do not drink or use, *no matter what.*
- Since drinking/using is not an option for us, we take whatever steps are necessary to continue our Sobriety Priority lifelong.
- We can achieve "the good life." However, life is also filled with uncertainties; therefore, we do not drink/use regardless of feelings, circumstances, or conflicts.
- We share in confidence with each other our thoughts and feelings as sober, clean individuals.
- Sobriety is our Priority, and we are each responsible for our lives and our sobriety.

Sam: There seems to be a lot of new faces here. Let's get acquainted! Please introduce yourselves, starting with my friend here on my right.

Norm: Norm, used-to user.
George: I'm George, a sober alcoholic.
Kyla: Hi, I'm Kyla. I overeat—or at least I did.
Joan: Joan, formerly habituated to booze and dope.
Hal: I'm Hal—long-time sober alcoholic.
Emma: Hello, I'm Emma and I'm a recovering alcoholic.
Mary: My name is Mary; I'm an old sober alcoholic.
Don: Don here—sober boozer.
Eric: I'm Eric, a clean pothead.
Susan: I answer to Susan, the sober alcoholic.
Janet: I'm Janet, an alcoholic new to sobriety.
Doug: Doug, practicing sobrietist.
Martin: I'm Martin and I'm a sober alcoholic.
Louise: This is Louise, the drunk who's sober now.
Kenneth: I am Kenneth and sobriety is my chief priority.
Sam: And I'm Sam, former alcoholic gone sober.

The meeting is now open. We have a large number of people here tonight—pretty impressive for a fledgling Tuesday night group. I'll bet some of you already attend a regular SOS meeting and are looking for another group to join. That's my hunch, so I'd like us all to get better acquainted. To give everyone ample chance to speak, I'd like to restrict crosstalk and commentary to the coffee-break (about midway through) and the optional restaurant conversation after the meeting. Coffee's always on in the rear of the room, but if you smoke, you have to go outside the building.

Now, perhaps today's topic could be, "What brought me to SOS?"

I'll begin, to get things started. I'm Sam, 43 years old, and sober for three years, two months. I was born and raised in Minnesota. I have one brother who lives there. My parents are deceased. . . . I left Minnesota when I was 21–22 for New York. At the time I was [set] on a career in the professional theater. . . .

Born in 1947. One of the baby boomers. Lived in several homes when I was very young. Someone told me we moved around quite a bit. My father was alcoholic. My mother divorced him when I was about five, I believe, and my younger brother was one. He evidently [became] late-stage alcoholic pretty fast. His deterioration from alcohol went fairly fast. He was in his thirties. He was typical of the skid-row alcoholic. He lived on the streets, he spent nights at the train yards. He was quite the chronic alcoholic. Since he left when I was so young, I don't have any recollection of things back that young—only what I've been told about restraining orders, and that kind of thing. Evidently when he drank he was a violent person.

For the most part I and my brother were raised by my mother. She remarried when I was about 11 years old to a nonalcoholic, but a sociopath. She stayed married to him for about four or five years, and then they divorced. Home life was pretty crazy in many ways: first alcoholism, then sociopathy, and my mother was queen of the martyrs. She was neurotic—[what] they would today call a codependent. Narcissistic and inappropriate with her children in the sense that, because I was very bright and very vocal at a very early age, I became her confidant, and her case manager, and her therapist, and so forth. . . .

We were sent to parochial schools during the fifties, which I wouldn't do to my worst enemy these days—sending a kid to a Catholic parochial school. It was a terrible place to go to school. The older nuns in the fifties were straight out of the Dark Ages. . . .

I was very independent as a child, I am told. . . . Went to high school in Minnesota, where I grew up. That's where I started drinking, in high school. I liked most of the alcoholics that I'd spoken with and definitely remembered the first time I used alcohol. I can remember thinking something to the effect that "Wherever you go now, My Life, this is wonderful!" During those high school years I did a lot of weekend drinking.

Since I work in a treatment center I spend a lot of time talking to alcoholics, and I'm convinced that I can take any alcoholic, including myself, and in the first year that they're drinking point out significant and substantial consequences from their drinking. Most of us don't talk about consequences till we get arrested, but the consequences start early, start immediately for an addict of any kind. Mine were starting already at that age. I was making decisions as to what I would do based on whether there would be drink in it. I was manipulating the company that I kept by whether or not they were drinkers or nondrinkers, or whether they drank like I did or not. I was making decisions as to what I would do with my limited funds based on how much alcohol I had to buy. My consequences started immediately, as I think they do with almost any addict.

By the time I graduated from high school in 1965, I was in the beginning stages of active alcoholism. I'd go to a university in Minnesota to get a major in theater. I spent four—almost five —years there, going to school on and off, working, going to school; take a quarter off, go back to work or school, and so forth. I never did finish at the university. I left before I graduated. I can look back and say that a lot of what happened to me was based on my drinking. A lot of my inability to complete assignments, my inability to stick through with things, to follow through with projects, to follow through with the university, was affected by my alcoholism and my drinking.

I'd married at 19 for the first time, and that marriage ended when I was 23. We [were] two children getting married, basically. She wasn't alcoholic, I was, although she had come from an alcoholic home. I look back at those years—really, all my years-- and I can see the effects of both my alcoholism as an independent entity, and the sort of ACOA tendencies, those characteristics of a child that came from an alcoholic family. I had those two things going for me. It was like the alcoholism took the dysfunctions I had from the ACOA things and really gave me a merry chase. I was not a very functional human being; I functioned because

I was bright enough to get by. I developed early on this image of competency. I pretty much convinced anybody that I was competent and got by, but on the inside there were terrible fears of being incompetent, of being inferior. I developed quite a good mask to convince people that I was OK.

Following that I worked in professional theater companies for the next five, six years. I started out as an actor/director in the creative side and ended up spending most of my time in the business side. I chose adminstration, because I ate on a much more regular basis that way. The theater was a perfect place to be an alcoholic. First, because drinking and drugging and so forth was just a part of the milieu—it was the background of almost everyone—it wasn't noticed as unusual behavior to be intoxicated. If you were intoxicated at certain [times] then it wasn't looked on very favorably, but most of the time you could get away with drinking to excess, because so many people around us did. So it suited my alcoholism quite well. It fit my other ACOA tendencies, dysfunctions, pretty well, too. It was a place that allowed me a lot of latitude and a lot of freedom which you don't have in the "normal" world. I had never gained any sense of personal responsibility; I had no role model for that. . . .

Working in the different theater companies, enjoying my drinking, getting away with a lot of things because of what I could do, not experiencing the real consequences that I probably would have had had I some sort of stable family life, I really didn't experience much in terms of second- or third-party consequences. I was experiencing the consequences of my own drinking: the hangovers were starting to get worse; I had a few alcohol-related car accidents, but I was never charged with anything. I had had an open-bottle violation by my early twenties. Consequences were getting more serious, but, of course, I didn't see any of that.

At about 25 I moved to New York City, really turned off by university people, and with an attitude that those who can, do; and those who can't, teach. . . . Probably the best part of living in New York City, for me, as an alcoholic, is I didn't have to get in a car. I could get on a subway at three o'clock in the morning, intoxicated, and so lucky I never got mugged on the way back home.

I started working in theaters in New York, and I was still able to function fairly well. . . . At one point I was listed as one of the five best theater managers in the country. That was the peak in my career.

I moved from New York City to Virginia to manage a professional theater company in residence. As far as I know, I'm the only person that had a faculty position at the university, without ever having earned a degree. I wanted a faculty position if I was going to work there, so they gave it to me. That was the peak of what my alcoholism would allow. I had risen as far as I could go—from there it was a downhill slide. I couldn't see it, because my drinking was picking up again.

I stayed in Virginia for two years. From there I moved to manage another theater. Stayed there for a couple of years. All the time my drinking is picking up. I met a girl in Virginia who moved in with me, and we stayed together for four, five years. She knew that I drank a lot, but she had no idea that I was an alcoholic. I had very few blackouts, which, maybe, kept me going longer that I might have. I don't know: it was never something that gave me any concern. But I was always in a state of financial trouble because of my drinking. I could go out and spend a lot of money, buying drinks for other people and buying drinks for myself, trying to hustle women, looking for prostitutes. Gwen and I in Virginia were always on the edge financially, even though at that time I was making pretty good money.

When I moved to Long Island for two years, my job skills really started to deteriorate. My hangovers were so bad, I'd come in in the morning, and it was all I could do to hold myself together for the first couple of hours. I couldn't drink in the morning, even though some people did to feel better. I would get ill if I did drink in the morning, so alcohol did not appeal to me then. I had to get to a point during the day where I felt well enough to hold down a drink—sometimes noon, or sometimes four o'clock in the afternoon. . . . While I was doing that I was doing the best I could in my job, which was second best as it actually turned out. Then I would go out and drink a lunch, and sit at lunch for an hour and a half, and then come back and kind of muddle through the afternoon, after having had a couple of drinks. I wasn't very collected. I wasn't doing very well.

Anyhow, I spent two years there, and then I moved to New Hampshire to manage a theater [there], where my drinking really picked up. In Long Island I had gone to see a psychiatrist, first. I was starting to get miserable. The alcoholic depression was getting pretty bad. I was not a happy puppy by any stretched imagination. . . . I've always had a problem with depression. A psychiatrist in New York City prescribed some antidepressant medication and a tranquilizer as well. I don't think that was a really good combination. First of all he asked me if I drank, and I said, "Well, you know, hardly at all, or just a little bit now and then," so he didn't know what was going on. I must have been a chemical mess at the time. The interaction between the drugs and the alcohol was really making me pretty screwy at times. I had managed that theater company for a year, and that was the first job I lost because of my alcoholism. I didn't lose it as a *direct* cause, I lost it as an indirect result. I just didn't do a very good job. . . . I got discharged, because I didn't do what I was supposed to do. At the time I thought it was a political this and a political that. I had all kinds of reasons why it couldn't have been because of me. In fact, actually it was.

The girl I was living with got a job in Boston. I was in New Hampshire, sixty miles north of Boston. We spent about the next nine months doing absolutely nothing, except drinking. And staying in the house. That's when I first started to notice these— sort of paranoid—didn't want to go out of the house, and I could stay in the house all day. Just didn't want to go out of the house. *I could.* When I had to I'd go out grocery shopping, or do whatever I had to do, but I didn't like leaving the house. I didn't think anybody was out there to get me, but I just didn't like to leave the house, certainly related to my drinking. I was buying vodka by the half-gallons, and by now I was just drinking vodka on the rocks instead of pretending that I was a martini drinker. I'd order martinis because it sounded better than ordering vodka on the rocks, but really, that's all I wanted, was on the rocks. Quickest way to get high that I knew of. So my drinking was picking up pretty good.

When relations moved to Boston, she and I stopped that commute. I sat around there for about six months, didn't do anything, and then I found a job in a theater company in Boston as the head of the educational services. . . . I'm on the downhill side of my career. I already had been for some time. I take this job, and I could do the job in about a half a day's work. A lot of time I'd pretend that I was out doing something else, but I'd really be in a bar somewhere. . . . I'd end up drinking, doing all kinds of financial things again. I'm taking this car to work instead of taking the subway, just because I don't like the trains in Boston—crowded and so on. So I'd drive this car about two miles down the road downtown. I'd park it in a garage, and it would cost me an awful lot of money just to park the car, but it was part of the alcoohlic grandiosity. About 1980, things were going very bad between this woman and myself. We hadn't had a relationship for about the last year; we just lived in the same household. I was still taking medication and drinking and doing all kinds of screwy—. I had a car accident that could have been fatal. I had been drinking. Gwen was out of town. I'm going to see a friend of mine who lived in Vermont. It was late in the evening, and there was a snowstorm. Highway's closed up, and they didn't let anyone out on the roads. Well, I was tanked up and wanted to go see this girl who lived in Vermont. I got in my car, started driving to Vermont, driving along the mountain roads, wondering why the hell everyone was driving so slow. I'm cranking along I suppose at fifty–sixty miles an hour. There's a little snow blowing around, but shit, no big deal, I come from

Minnesota, I know what snow's all about. I can't figure it out why these damn cars are going so slow. The road looked pretty OK to me. I can see the line—no problem.

Next thing I do is crash into a guardrail. I crashed into a snowbank and hit a guardrail, and my car went up on the guardrail and kind of perched on top of the guardrail. The whole thing is a mystery to me. I still don't know how it happened. I just kind of nodded off. All of a sudden I'm sitting on top of a guardrail. I get out of the car and step on the road, slipped, fell on my ass. The road is sheer ice. I thought it looked fine. It was like a skating rink. Now I understood why people were going so slow. I perched on top of this guardrail on top of the snowbank, and the guardrail was next to a drop, probably, of two–three hundred feet into a ravine. I could have gone over the top of that hill so easily and been down at the bottom of that ravine. It was that close.

I must have really looked intoxicated. Although I don't know, I was in a three-piece suit at the time. A guy took me to a small town, dropped me off at a motel, and told me where they were going to tow the car. That's how I made arrangements the next day to get the car fixed and to stay there for a couple of days, and go back to New Hampshire. There were no legal consequences of the accident. Didn't stop drinking.

We moved to Boston and got this apartment there for a while, and Gwen came home one day and announced that she had had some experiences and decided that she was gay, and that that was going to be her lifestyle. That sort of set me back, but I was drinking so heavily that it affected me and yet it didn't affect me. Everything was in a fog at this point I was drinking so heavily. I was barely managing to do the educational director job at this theater company. Rather than having any of my own feelings about what was going on, I was trying to counsel her through this transition of hers. I remember I did have some jealousy. She would invite girlfriends over to the house, and I had this memory of hanging out this third-floor window of my apartment, [tumbler] of vodka in my hand, trying to hear what they're saying on the balcony.

Then I knew that the job at the theater company wasn't going to last, so I called my mother who had at one time alluded to the fact that I drank too much. She talked about what was available [in] treatment. I knew I had to get out of Boston. Couldn't live with Gwen anymore. The job wasn't working out very well. I didn't have enough money to move into a new apartment. I was really stuck for something to do. So I remember calling her and saying, "You know what? I think I'll try this alcohol treatment. That sounded pretty good." What it really was was a way for me to get out of Boston. I knew I had to sober up long enough to figure out what the hell I was going to do next. I flew out to Minnesota, and left most of my stuff in Boston in the apartment. The day I left I can remember—I don't think I drank that day—but I spent most of the day crying. It was a miserable experience. I had realized what shape I was in. . . .

Got off to Minnesota and stayed for a week until they had an opening at a treatment facility. I didn't know anything about the treatment, didn't know what the hell I was getting into. I really didn't even think I was an alcoholic. I just needed a place to hide out, and this was going to be like a thirty-day paid vacation. I went through detox without too much trouble. Spent a couple of days on a detox unit and then I went into a treatment unit. The next two weeks I just kind of walked around and watched what the hell was going on, trying to make sense out of all this. Finding the lectures interesting and just sitting in groups and not participating. I was trying to figure out what was going on. I'm a controller by nature, I like to have things under control. If I don't know what's going on I'm very uncomfortable. So I sat around until I figured out what was going on. We had to do a story there, as I suppose they do in many treatment centers. You tell your story. I watched several people do that exercise, and mine was a very good literary exercise. It had nothing to do with my feelings about being alcoholic, because I didn't have any at that time, but I was going to play the game very well, so it became a literary masterpiece, a most wonderful little story that didn't mean shit. I learned how to play the game in there, although I think my inability to address feelings—to understand feelings, to be involved with feelings—was the reason they recommended me for their extended-care program. Which was fine with me, because I still didn't know what the hell I was going to do next.

I was starting to get into the therapy aspects of what was going on. I found I still had needs that weren't being met—that have really never been met physically—things that were the result of my upbringing and the dysfunctions I had from really having to do things on my own for the most part. The therapy part of this program appealed to me. I wanted some answers, and I wanted to understand these depressions. I did have a psychiatric consultation after I had been there for some time, and the psychiatrist put me back on the antidepressant medication. He was the first one with whom I had spent any time talking about the history of the depressions and the alcoholism. He was the first who suggested that in addition to the alcoholism I had a problem with depression that might be able to be treated with medication. That was his feeling. They weren't big on giving out medication at the treatment center, so there had to be a legitimate reason for it. He put me on the antidepressant medication.

I spent the next four months in their extended-care facility. The noise that I did make was that I was an atheist. The first time I ran across these 12 steps and higher power business I said, "What do I do? I'm an atheist. I've been an atheist since I was in the ninth grade. None of this makes any sense to me." We had lectures—and sometimes good ones—on the disease concept of alcoholism and I said to my counselor, "You tell me that I have this disease, and now you're telling me I have to have a religious conversion in order to recover from this disease. This makes no sense to me whatsoever." He told me I had better learn to get a higher power or I wasn't going to stay sober. I was told that by several people there, including another psychiatrist that I saw for a while there. The first psychiatrist I had seen was a Unitarian, so he was kind of take it or leave it. He said, "Well, you know people are . . . confused. So you go to these things and then you go with what you need and leave the rest." He was a pretty rational guy. . . . I stayed there working on things other than higher powers for some time. We had all kinds of groups, and I think I did get some treatment that was productive.

This is also when I was introduced, interestingly enough, to Rational Emotive Therapy. At the time, 1980, this was big stuff. At Hazelden they were using RET pretty heavily. They had these RET groups. Yeah, I picked it up in a big way. I look back at it now and I realize I took to it because it was a mistake in the ensuing years. Since I have a degree in psychology and I'm fairly well read in the field, I see now what I was doing. Rational Emotive Therapy is for a person like myself, who was out of touch with his emotions, was a regressor of emotions. Rational Emotive Therapy is a perfect place to hide, because you don't have to have any emotions. All you need to do is have some perfect sentence structure. If you feel the way you talk, then all you got to do is improve your talk and you'll feel just wonderful. It's this rational, logical system that's based on language. . . . It was perfect. That's all that mental health is about—talking to yourself properly. Well, then I would learn how to talk to myself properly, and everything should be great. So I became a junior little RET counselor and helped everybody talk to themselves appropriately. Quite funny.

I met a woman when I was there. The extended-care unit had opened this, not a coed, a men's and a women's unit. But I met a woman there and, boy, we really hit it off pretty good. She was older than myself by about eight years. I was 32 at the time, I think. She was 40. We hit it off in a big way. Had a relationship in treatment and got thrown out.

I know several people who were in treatment who'd gone out and relapsed, snuck out and gone down the road and gotten drunk, or had pills smuggled in, or whatever. If they did that in treatment, the policy was that they sent them back to the detox unit and until they could "arrange for transfer to another facility"— another treatment center. That was standard procedure if you relapsed. They didn't want you to stay there because they thought that a relapse without consequence wasn't very good, so they sent you to another treatment center. When Cynthia and I were caught having a relationship, we were gone, off the property within two hours. It was really quite strange. All I remember is a couple of hours later we were standing in the airport looking for each other. That's where they dropped us off, with no kind of aftercare plan, no suggestion as to what to do next. My counselor was so mad at me, he gave me a sheet of paper—I still have it— with these recommendations on it, in BIG letters: It said, "You'd better find yourself a higher power." It was all he could think of to say as I was leaving: "You've goddam well better find your-self a higher power."

We'd violated their moral code, and violating the moral code made us worse than alcoholics in their eyes. There's no explana-tion I can come up with for how cruelly we were treated. I was under psychiatric care at the time. I was never allowed to see a psychiatrist before we left. We were just given the bum's rush, put in a station wagon, dropped off at the airport, and that was it. Terribly unprofessional. Very unprofessional.

So this woman said to me, "Look, I've got a house in Florida. What're you doing?" And I said, "Well, I've got no place to go. I can't go back to my mother's place. That's unacceptable. I've really got no place to go." She said, "Well, you should come down with me, down to Florida." So I said "Yes."

We flew down to Florida. She was on her second treatment at the time I'd been through the treatment and had internalized some values about sobriety, and I had been five months sober while I was in treatment. The first couple of months I knew I would drink again, there was no doubt in my mind. Giving up drinking was a crazy idea. But by the time I left I really had gotten the idea that I was an alcoholic, and that sobriety actually was probably the way to go. I was pretty gung-ho at first when we arrived in Florida. I realized that I needed help—could not do it by myself. I went to some of the AA clubs and they were just horrible, as bad as they get. It was bible-thumping, "Big Book"-thumping *AA!* If you said anything to the effect of you didn't use a higher power you were just ostracized. That was all there was to it.

Cynthia, the one I moved down with, she's not going to meetings with me. She said, "Listen, I just can't take it." One of the reasons I think we hit it off is that she too was agnostic or just a nonbeliever. She said, "I can't get into this higher power stuff. It's just ridiculous." She stopped going to meetings because of that. I kept going to meetings because I figured I had to have something. I went down to the central office of AA, and I said, "Look, can I start a group, and put it in your name? I've got an atheist or agnostic group, just so I can meet some people who are like myself." He said, "No, you can't do that. That's basic. Go try this group. I think there's a bunch of atheists in this." This is where I found the secular AA group that had been meeting for quite some time.

Walking in there is like being welcomed into a family. It was quite a nice group of people. Many of them are still in my life today. They were very welcoming, very open. We found a place that we could feel at home. Now, we made several classic mistakes. We were warned by people not to make our recovery or our alcoholism a "we" problem, but that's exactly what we did. "Our" sobriety. It wasn't mine and it wasn't hers. "Our sobriety." It was "our this" and "our that." And we didn't have a very happy relationship at the time. I lasted six months, and then I had a relapse that lasted about a weekend. [I ran] back to AA, telling everybody what had happened, and stayed sober for about six months; then I relapsed again.

After that first year, my relapses got closer and closer together. But the next eight years really [brought] me in and out, in and out of AA. I'd be drunk for a while, and then I'd sober up for a while. Drink for three months, sober up for a month or two. Maybe I could pull through four months of sobriety, then I'd want to go back and start drinking again. After a certain period of time, I had made some friends in AA—acquaintances, I should say really. And I was trying to be honest with people about what was going on with me, and I mentioned that I was on this medication. Of course, I was told by everyone that I talked to that that was a no-no. "If you're on antidepressant medication, you aren't sober," "You aren't clean," or "Something's wrong with you."

I'm embarrassed to say that I kind of bought it. I started thinking about it, "Maybe I can do without it. I didn't really need them anyhow." So I went off the medication, and stayed off it for the next eight years. I look back now and I think that was a big, big mistake, to have just dropped the medication. Now I recognize the fact that I really am one of those who is diagnosed as alcoholic. Alcoholism is an independent entity. I also had dysthmia [mood disorder] as an independent entity, also, that needs to be treated with medication. I'm on medication now and have been for the last three years. I really feel victimized by what I found in AA at the time, by the attitude that (1) if I didn't have a higher power I couldn't stay sober, and (2) that if I was seeing a psychiatrist and I was on medication, there was something wrong with me. That I wasn't within the program. It was so outrageous and so nonproductive.

My ex and I spent the next eight years on and off. She'd get sober, I'd get sober. She'd drink, I'd drink; I'd drink, she'd drink. This was one of the most miserable existences I could imagine. There's absolutely nothing worse than sitting in a bar, drinking, wishing you were sober. It's just a miserable, miserable feeling.

I would say, "Come on!" I'd get sober again, I'd go back to AA—to the secular AA group—and I would try, three months, four months. I'd hang in there. There was some very good sobriety there. But between my depression and my inability to deal with my own emotions at the time, it didn't work. I'd go out drinking again. The woman I had come down with had a great deal of money at the time. We didn't work. We went to AA, and we tried to stay sober, and then we'd travel—we did a lot of traveling at the time. It could have been wonderful if it wasn't ruined by the alcohol. We won a free trip to Europe. Spent four months traveling around Europe on Eurail passes. What I remember about that trip are some of the horrible drunks that I got into. So in 1988 I got sober on June 30.

I was living on a boat at the time, and I had woke up that morning hung over after a typical night's drinking. Felt miserable, but no more miserable than I did most mornings when I got up with a hangover. But something that day inside me said, "This is enough. I don't want to do this anymore. I can't live like this anymore. I've had it. I've had it. I don't want to do this anymore." That night I had my last two drinks and have been sober since that date.

I went into an outpatient program in Florida, where I was, I thought, handled pretty well. The counselor I had wasn't big on the 12 Steps. She encouraged me to keep doing things in a secular fashion if that's what I wanted to. She put me in several groups that helped considerably. Family [oriented] groups where I could work out some things. I got put in several of what they called at the time "feelings groups," where I got a chance to exercise in group feeling-oriented things. Learned how to get in touch with my own feelings, and so forth. About six months into that process, I was still feeling kind of stuck and unhappy and depressed. My counselor felt by that time I should have been feeling better, so she sent me off to another psychiatrist for an evaluation. And that psychiatrist put me on medication, antidepressant medication. About two months later I really did pick up and start to feel good about what I was doing, feel good about being sober. At that time I had some money in the bank. The first year of my recovery I didn't work. I just lived off my savings. I look back now, I wasn't really capable of working. I was really still pretty much a mess that first year. I remember in the past, I would hear people at meetings say, "Oh yeah, that first year's really rough!" and "Damn! That first year was really something!" In my sort of ignorance and arrogance I would say, "Well, when I get sober, it won't be like that for me. It won't be that way for me. I'll just talk to myself right and everything will be hunky-dory."

That first year was pretty damn tough! I was up and down, all over the place, and really working hard. I would [do] things I never dreamed I would do. I did art therapy for six months, with a therapist, and I'm drawing pictures and trying to get feelings. I did pretty much anything they would suggest that was working in the direction of recovery. They told me to go to art therapy, I went to art therapy. They told me to do some silly things, I did some silly things just to do them, because they told me to do them. I wanted to get sober. I did not want to go back to drinking.

I first got a copy of *How to Stay Sober* when I was in counseling. I remember reading it and saying, "Well, at last somebody's doing something! What's going on here?" We had the secular AA group for some time, but that was actually going in a direction that I didn't like. It was really a personality group that was run by a couple who had made their intellectual claim in the sixties to behaviorism. Like B. F. Skinner, they probably thought only they were conscious, and the rest of the world simply did things for reward, and they didn't allow much emotional talk to go on in their meetings. The general semantics movement, that same real cognitive sort of talk and linguistically oriented therapy wasn't what I needed at all, so I didn't go to that group at that time, because I needed something else. . . .

[My friend] Steve had come down to see me and told me that they just started this SOS group. I immediately joined that group and I've been going to that group ever since. I needed to make a commitment to sobriety and starting other SOS meetings was one of my ways of doing it, as was just showing up at the new SOS meeting every Wednesday night no matter what. If anybody came, that was great. If they didn't, that was OK, too. I was still doing some work to stay sober. I've since started another group that's taking off quite well. . . .

One of the things about SOS that I think is most productive [is] that we see sobriety as learning what your needs are and then learning how to meet them; and if you have a problem that demands some work, some therapy, whatever it is, then you go out and you find your appropriate source, and you get your needs met. If that means psychiatry, then you go to psychiatry. If that means some kind of other counseling, then you go to that kind of counseling. If it was marriage counseling, you go to marriage counseling. But you find what you need and you go out and you meet your needs. AA expects that all your needs can only be met by the 12 Steps of AA, and that everyone else is suspect: physicians are suspect, psychiatrists are suspect; counselors are suspect. Anyone who's not in AA is suspect. Of course, that is one of the primary qualities of a cult. In that sense AA is very much a cult. They see all other self-help groups, even [those] that deal with alcohol, as threats to their system.

All my real long-term sober time is in SOS. I never had any long-term sober time in AA, and the people in SOS helped me a great deal. They were rational, they were caring. That's where this group works so much better than that other secular AA group, because these guys aren't afraid to talk about their feelings. That's what human beings do. So everything came together for me at a time when I needed it. . . . I ran into the people who started the SOS group here, and I was in a place where it was time for me to get sober. I was ready. I was sick and tired of being sick and tired. . . .

Sam: If anything I said sounded familiar or rang a bell with any of you, please share it with us. Janet?

Janet: I'm Janet, I'm 33 years old, and I've been sober for twenty-six months. I was born in California. I have an older brother who's two years older than I am, and a younger brother who's four years younger than I am. My parents divorced when I was eight, and before they divorced, my mom was in and out of the hospital. She was not drinking but she was using pills and prescription medication. There was a lot of fighting and a lot of things going on between my parents, and I became sort of the caretaker of the family. My older brother and I, we sort of took over the roles, actually, of father and mother, and took care of my little brother, trying to protect him from the strife that was going on. When my parents divorced, my mom started drinking and spent a lot of time out at bars. So my brother and I sort of continued taking care of things and making sure that each other got to school and had lunch made, and all that kind of stuff.

I guess I was 11 when Mom remarried, to a man who had three children who were the same ages as my brothers and I. At that point, we had six kids—kind of like the "Brady Bunch" in the sense of the ages of the children—and mom and my ex-stepfather argued from the start and drank a lot.

Up until about 11, I had sipped beer from my dad's can, but when Mom remarried and there was a lot of tension between her and my ex-stepfather and the children added to the household, we were allowed to have wine on certain occasions. There was so much drinking going on that it was not hard to sneak some here and sneak some there, and I discovered that it immediately made me—I thought it made me—feel better. That marriage lasted for about seven years, and during that time there were the usual teeenage parties. There were drugs there, but I wasn't interested. I tried marijuana, but it didn't do what alcohol seemed to do for me—take away my feelings.

At the age of 17 I went to Germamy as an exchange student and there I discovered schnapps and beer. To me, that was the beginning of the end, the beginning of my drinking on a regular basis. I drank daily and discovered that I could keep up with the best of them and, in fact, drink more than the best of them. I thought I was maintaining myself, and I spent a summer there. When I came back, Mom's second marriage was splitting up. When I came back I still was only 17, I wasn't old enough to buy liquor.

My older brother wasn't either, but he would buy it for the two of us and we would drink. I'd also get into my mom's liquor supply and take half of it out and fill half of it with water and drink to put myself to sleep at night, because there was a lot going on, again, with her marriage. All during this time I somehow managed to [be a] straight-A student, section leader of the flute section of the marching band, an exchange student, and homecoming princess—all that stuff. On the outside I tried to make it look like we were a normal family, and I was a normal person, and I was achieving great things, and I was preparing for college; meanwhile, I was drinking, not the amounts that I drank toward the end of my drinking but drinking an awful lot on a daily basis.

I started college, junior college. By this time my mom was becoming really nonfunctional. Between alcohol and prescription pills we just never knew if we'd find her passed out when we got home. Suicide attempts: I found her a couple of times. My older brother and I continued to drink, and at this point my younger brother was probably fourteen and he came home from a couple of parties bombed, and that upset me. It didn't upset me that I was drinking; it didn't upset me that my older brother was drinking; but it upset me that my younger brother was drinking.

Anyway, I went through the two years of junior college and continued to drink. I then transferred to a university and moved out of my mom's house. I rented a room from my aunt. My aunt is my father's sister, and a heavy drinker as it turned out. I was on a student loan and scholarship and working and I couldn't afford more than—my focus (when I was home) was with trying to figure out how I was going to drink. When I was at school I was still managing to achieve pretty good grades, and I was working, and I was in the university's marching band. Everything on the outside looked like everything was fine. But at home I was drinking. . . . When I lived with my aunt, I couldn't afford more than—I was buying those big big boxes of wine and jugs of wine and keeping them in my closet in my bedroom. But my aunt had things like ouzo and Pernod and we'd sit around the fire-place and we'd drink that.

My drinking continued and then at the age of 22 I married and became a teacher, taught junior high. I had a real hard time doing the teaching. I did a good job of it—again I managed on the outside to look like everything was fine—and I managed to do an excellent job, but it was becoming more and more diffi-cult to get up and go to work in the morning and get through a workday without drinking. Four hours into my workday my hands would start to shake and I thought that I needed a drink, and I couldn't deal with that too well, but I managed. As soon as I hit the door, though, I drank. My ex-husband drank, too, although he didn't drink nearly as much as I did.

After two years of teaching junior high, I tired of teaching that level, and I went into a private school teaching four- and five-year-olds. At that point I could not make it through a workday without drinking. I had to drink in the morning to get going and to get rid of the shakes, and I would literally just about fall apart if I couldn't have a drink somewhere in the day. I started bringing my alcohol to work and hiding it, putting it in a coffee mug and putting things into it, trying to hide it. That continued for some time.

When I started drinking at work I also started falling down at work. I missed meetings. At home I drank even more. At work I drank first to maintain myself—what I thought was maintaining myself; at home I'd pass out. I blacked out, I fell down stairs, I split my head open, I ripped my knees open. I was vomiting every morning and sometimes in the afternoons, yet I was continuing to drink. I had to allow myself an extra hour every morning when I got up because I had to allow the time to get sick to my stomach, throw up, and then to get alcohol into my system and see if I could get that down. I was basically self-medicating. I was really trying not to feel anything and at that point I knew I was an alco-holic, and I didn't know how to stop. I was terrified of stopping, I was terrified of my continued drinking, I was just terrified.

It was being in between a rock and a hard place. I was really scared of what I was doing to myself, and yet I didn't know how I could stop, and I didn't know how I could live without drinking. My marriage was miserable, and I didn't have the strength anymore to do anything. My self-esteem was really low. I constantly felt guilty about my drinking—and at that point I was drinking almost twenty-four hours a day. I could not maintain a job at the private school: I was never accused of drinking, but I was just told I wasn't doing my job. I was being fired for the first time in my life, and I knew why. I was full of despair. Because I had a contract, they said they'd continue my paychecks if I would leave. Apparently, I was really making a spectacle of myself, and here I thought I was maintenance drinking. But then I had a good six months of paychecks coming in from this job that I wasn't even going to; I could stay home and really drink. In a twenty-four-hour period, I was going through a 1.75-liter bottle. It became very expensive. I lived to drink and I drank to live, and yet, underneath it all, I really kind of wanted to die, and I knew that too, and that was scary.

After that money ran out, financially it became a hardship. I wasn't working, and no paychecks were coming in, and I didn't know how in the world I was going to have a job. Things were going really bad between my ex and me, emotionally and financially, and he couldn't stand it when I got drunk. On the other hand he couldn't stand it when I tried not to drink, because if I tried not to drink for more than an hour I'd turn into a witch, and he'd go and get me the alcohol because I was so hard to live with. I found a job—so that I could appease him, really—teaching pre-school, but it was every other day. I chose a job with another teacher, so I only had to work a partial day, till one o'clock; yet I still had to drink there. I had to drink before I got there, and I drank once I got there. I brought it with me, and I felt horribly guilty again: here I am teaching little children, little toddlers, and I'm drinking. There was a kitchen opposite the classroom and I'd pop in there and drink.

Through all of this, I knew I was an alcoholic, I just knew it. I read practically everything that I could find on it, until I couldn't read any more, couldn't focus enough to read. And I watched programs and I saw people on TV talking about how wonderful it was to be clean and sober and how many days they had or how many weeks they had and I just couldn't even believe it because I thought, "You do this thing one day at a time? I couldn't go an hour! I just couldn't." It just seemed impossible to me. Finally I got to the point where I was physically very, very ill, and I went to different doctors, too. It's amazing: not one doctor ever said to me, "Do you drink?" I went to one doctor because I was vomiting blood, and he said, "Well, it's probably an ulcer" and prescribed ulcer medication which I obviously couldn't take very well because that made me sick, too.

I was in and out of emergency hospital because I was constantly falling down and cutting myself open and needing stitches and then not remembering it. Only one emergency room doctor ever said anything, and he didn't ask me if I drank, he asked my ex-husband, "Was she drinking, and how much did she have?" My ex said, "Yes, she was drinking, and I have no idea. . . ."

I knew I was physically ill, but I didn't realize how ill I was. What I did know was that I was sick and I was tired and I was sick and tired of being sick and tired, and I felt like there was no point in going on living. I finally had made up my mind that I would die by the age of 45 from my alcoholism, and that would be the end of it. On the other hand, I couldn't stand that thought either. A rock and a hard place.

Dying from alcoholism was too slow; yet I didn't have the courage to do anything faster. I discovered that somewhere a little tiny part of me didn't want to die, and I became a little bit scared of dying. My mother—actually my younger brother—confronted me and said, "We're just worried." At this point I wasn't invited to any family functions, because there was always a lot of drinking and I always drank the most, and I always ended up picking a fight with someone and creating a scene. I was really isolated from my family, I stopped talking to my friends, and I was still doing this preschool job, somehow. But a two-week break in between sessions was coming up, and my mom and brother said, "What can we do to help you out?" I said, "I don't know. I honestly don't know." And they didn't mention my drinking per se, they just said, "We see that you're sad, and we don't know what to do." I said, "Well, the only thing I know, the only person I know who might be able to help me is this [one] doctor." The thought of going to AA or any other group program made me laugh—I saw them on TV, I heard them talking about one day—one day at a time was incomprehensible to me.

I went to the doctor actually thinking, "Well, I'm depressed, and if I weren't so depressed maybe I wouldn't drink so much. If he can help me with my depression then maybe I won't need to drink like this and I can drink like a normal person." So I went to him and told him I was sleeping, but most of the time I was drinking, and I wasn't eating much at all. I described all this to him, and he listened, and he was the first doctor to ever directly ask me, "Do you drink alcohol?" I said, "Yes," and then he said, "How much?" I said, "I don't even know." Then he started listing amounts. "One drink a night? Two drinks a night? Three drinks a night? Four drinks a night?" And I'm thinking and I said, "It's not *a* night. It's all the time. It's whenever I'm awake, I'm drinking, and if I'm not awake then I'm unconscious, because I've had so much to drink." That was the first time I'd ever admitted to anyone—said out loud—how much I was consuming, and I didn't even get into exactly how much, just the fact that it was an overwhelming situation.

I still wasn't thinking that I was going to quit drinking. I was thinking that I was just going to be treated for depression and then drink like a normal person and not drink alcoholically. I kind of thought, at that point, an alcoholic could control his or her drinking. The doctor made it clear to me that he couldn't treat my depression while I was drinking, because he could not tell where the drinking began and ended and where the depression began and ended when they were so intertwined. He strongly suggested that I go into a detox [center], which absolutely *terrified* me. The thought of not drinking for—he was talking about ten days. The thought of that was—, it was—. I said "I can't do that," and I resisted, and he said, "You're almost nonfunctional, and you're going to be nonfunctional soon if you don't do this."

So I had to think about that. I went home and thought about it. This program was very expensive, and I didn't know what to do, and I didn't know if I could do it, and I knew I couldn't afford it. Ironically, my mom ended up offering to pay. Actually, her husband was so concerned about the family situation that he was going to pay. I was terrified of the hospital because of my mom being in and out when I was a child, but I finally decided I was going to do this, that I would go through with this program, but when I got out then I was going to go ahead and drink again.

I was 31 years old, and I went into the hospital to detox, and I had my last drink the night before, with my family. My last drink *out* with the family—when I came home I had more, even though the doctor said it would be easier if I didn't get completely drunk the night before I went in the hospital. I didn't actually get bombed, but I did drink, and I went in the next morning and began detoxing. It was a scary experience, and I hadn't realized how physically ill I was. The doctor had a liver specialist come and look at me. He did blood work and [found] I had malnutrition and jaundice and hepatitis and my liver was so inflamed that when the doctor touched the outside of my abdomen I jumped. I was just really, really physically ill, but I couldn't stay in the hospital. I just could not stand being in there.

I was introduced to AA when I was in the hospital. The doctor sent someone to come and talk with me, and she took me to a noon AA meeting, and I left through half of it. I could not stand it. She stayed through the rest of the meeting because she's an alcoholic herself, a sober alcoholic; I went back to the floor. AA wasn't going to fix it for me either. Nothing was going to fix it for me. However, by the second day, about forty-eight hours after I had no alcohol in my system, I realized that I wasn't going to be able to drink again and live. It just became clear as a bell to me, that I had to make a choice, that it was up to me, that I was not going to be able to come out of that hospital and control my drinking, because drinking would control me again. I had to decide if I was going to live or if I was going to die, because if I wanted to drink I was going to die, and if I wanted to live I had to live sober, and so I had to do some soul-searching and decide how much of me really wanted to live and give living a thought. Living and feeling: all these years of drinking I had been trying not to feel. I decided to try to live sober. I also decided that the hospital was making me feel even more anxious than I needed to feel, and instead of staying the ten days I asked if I could be released so I could recover at home. The doctor wasn't real thrilled about that, but he said, "Well, then, try it." I think, in the back of his mind, he thought I just wanted to just get out and drink again.

Anyway, after two-and-a-half days I was released—actually, I just released myself. I went home, and my ex-husband had cleaned out all the liquor in the house, so there was no alcohol in the house. I spent that first day at home thinking, "I can't do this by myself, I can't stay sober by myself. I need some help with this." I went to an AA meeting, and it was huge, one of those enormous meetings where there were probably 300 people. I couldn't even last the whole meeting. It was a speaker meeting, and the speaker was cheerfully telling his story of sobriety and it just didn't make any sense to me. I was really having a hard time. I was going not one hour at a time, but about every ten minutes at a time, struggling not go to out and drink.

I went back to the doctor, and I spoke to him, "I need a group." He said, "Try another AA meeting. I know that they're not all the same." So I tried another AA meeting, and I liked it better, but I still didn't feel comfortable; yet I knew that I needed some help. But the thought of turning my life over to a higher power at that point made no sense to me. What I needed to know was, "How can I get through the next twenty minutes without a drink?" The steps, and being a baby, and being sponsored, and getting a cake—all that stuff was just hoopla to me. It wasn't going to help me get through the next twenty minutes.

When I went back to the doctor, I said, "I don't think I can do this, because I'm doing this alone, and I just don't see how I can do it." The doctor gave me some literature on SOS, and I thought, "Well, it can't hurt." So I called Jim Christopher, and went to my first SOS meeting. I was without alcohol in my system, but I was certainly still very dazed and confused and white-knuckling every minute. At the SOS meeting, I found some people who were very supportive, who gave me some strength to get through, not just every twenty minutes, but every hour; then I managed to make it to meeting to meeting.

I was still very angry: that I couldn't drink and live, that I had to make this choice. I was very angry about that. And I was very angry every time someone in the meeting said "It gets better." On one hand I was very angry because I thought, "No, it can't get better." On the other hand, I saw a ray of hope, because I saw people with time—sober time—who were saying this. That little part of me grabbed onto that and said, "It can get better? Maybe it really can," even though I didn't quite believe it. When people started talking about Sobriety Priority, I couldn't understand that for the life of me. I just couldn't figure that one out. Yet I heard it, and heard it, and heard it, and heard it, and I saw what it was doing for people in the group, and so I continued with the meetings. Amazingly, in the beginning I could not do anything without associating it with alcohol: I couldn't get up in the morning without thinking about a drink; I couldn't even brush my teeth without thinking about a drink. I couldn't do *anything without thinking about a drink.* Everything I did was associated with drinking or with hiding the bottles or with deciding on which store I am going to go to this time. I found that I had a lot of time on my hands, now that I wasn't spending all that time and energy drinking.

Soon afterwards, within three months of my sobriety, I was offered a teaching job at the level I had always [wanted] to teach. I was terrified of taking that job, thinking "If I take this job I may feel so much pressure that I may—. How am I going to teach without drinking?" I associated teaching with drinking, and how [was] I going to do that? With the encouragement of my doctor and the SOS group, I decided to take a healthy risk, for the first time. I took the job and discovered that I could do it. The more things I did without drinking, and the more support I got from the group and from my doctor, the less I started associating drinking with my behavior, with my activities, with my life. And the Sobriety Priority started to make sense to me: if I separate my drinking from all the other stuff and everything else that happens, then it becomes unnecessary for me to take a drink.

The first year of my sobriety was a year of hurt. New Year's Eve without alcohol? I spent it with SOS members and had a wonderful time, and discovered I could go to a party and not drink. I was angry on my birthday because I couldn't have champagne. So instead of going out and having the nice dinner that I was offered, I stayed home and ate a bowl of oatmeal, because I was really angry that I still couldn't drink. Every day was like coming out of a cocoon after ten years or more. Every day I started to notice things, and every day, all of a sudden, the sky was blue, and I hadn't noticed that for a long time. I discovered that I could laugh again, and that I had a sense of humor, and that the little things that happen in each day need to be appreciated, because if they're not it becomes difficult to be a happy person. The first year was a year of firsts. I also spent that year examining my marriage in a sober light and discovering that it wasn't where I should be; but I also felt that I should give it a shot, as a sober person, since I'd been drinking during the entire marriage. I gave it more than a year, and grew stronger physically. I became physically well. I worked with my doctor, and I worked with my SOS group. I discovered who I was, and that I had a lot more strength than I thought I had. I also kept very

busy with my new job teaching and loving every minute of it—
well not every minute, but as many minutes as one enjoys of
one's job.

I left my ex-husband. It was cause for fear in my family
when I moved into my own apartment at about fifteen or sixteen
months of sobriety. My family was concerned that because I was
by myself and living in my own place I would drink again. I knew
I wouldn't do that, because I don't feel I have another recovery
in me. I feel that if I were to drink again, to drink would mean,
for me, to die. At this point I had discovered so much—that
life is so thrilling and exciting and painful and difficult and
exhilarating and upsetting that I want to be here. I want to be
here and I want to feel the pain and I want to feel the joy. The
thought of drinking just because I was by myself was not an option for me. I was thrilled to be by myself—on my own, sober,
healthy, and with a good job and my own place to be.

When I decided that being sober is wonderful, I also had
decided that I was no longer angry that I couldn't drink. I had
accepted that it is a disease that I can't drink alcohol, but I can
do anything—everything—I want to do basically, if I'm not drinking. I needed to just take one day at a time and enjoy my life
and myself. I discovered that I really am a good person and that
I enjoyed being by myself and with myself, and that there's a
difference between being lonely and being alone, and that I was
not lonely, I was alone. . . .

Sobriety is life. If we're not sober we can't—we don't—
live. If we're not sober we can't have what we have with each
other and we can't have each day one day at a time. The one
day at a time now makes sense to me. It's one of the things
that threw me from the beginning: one was one day at a time;
the other was separating my sobriety from everything else, from
all this shit. Those are the two things that really keep me sober,
the two, let's say, basic threads of the fabric. We do live one
day at a time. We have to plan ahead just like every other person
does, and we have to schedule events, and we have to do certain

things, but what we really truly honest-to-God do—and it sounds
so corny, and probably a newcomer would do the same thing
I did and want to puke hearing this—is we do live one day at
a time, and we appreciate (I'm saying "we" now, but I'll speak
for myself) I appreciate being alive every single day. Every day
that I get up I am so grateful to be here, and everything that's
around me I *notice*. I notice things now. The world just began
to bloom for me. I notice the green trees and I notice that pile
of dirt in the corner. I notice everything. And I just revel in the
fact that I'm here and I'm alive and I'm sober.

I have my down days, just like everybody else, and I have
difficulties in my life, and I have pain in my life, and I have
joy in my life, and the thing is is that I'm able to feel all of
those things as wonderful. I wouldn't want not ever again to feel.
Certainly it's become easier and easier and, as time goes on, the
fewer things I associate with alcohol. In fact I don't associate any
of my activities with alcohol anymore. It's not that it doesn't cross
my mind. It's not that there aren't times when I think, "God,
it would be kind of nice to check out for a while, and not think
about things." But instead of checking out with alcohol I'll go
swimming or I'll talk about it with the group or with my family.

I have also found that in order to stay sober relatively comfortably, which I do at this point, I've just started calling it in
my mind, "spreading my sobriety around." I don't rely on any
one thing to keep me sober. It's a lot of things that I do to
stay sober. Sometimes it's a hot bath. Other times it's a long
talk. Sometimes it's a bowl of ice cream, which is really nice.
A lot of the times it's sitting and talking with other sober alcoholics, or talking with an alcoholic who's not sober. I do not
self-flagellate, I don't punish myself for what my life was or what
I did, but I do remind myself on a daily basis of where I was,
of the pain I felt, of the degradation. . . . Somebody will talk
about being sick, and I'll remind myself of when I had to vomit
every day. It's not something that I dwell on. I don't sit and
get on the pity pot about it, but I remind myself that that's what

my life was when I drank. And then I remind myself of where I am now, and how I feel now, how good I feel most of the time. Life is good—really good—and it's wonderful, and it's only wonderful because I'm sober, and it wouldn't be if I weren't.

Sam: Thank you for your story, Janet, and thank you for reminding us of something that's easy to forget.

I think Eric has something to share with us. Eric?

Eric: Eric at 42 has been sober nearly six years. I'm the third of a family of six kids: two older sisters, a brother a year younger, and then two younger sisters. The favorite memories that I have of that early period in my life are living out in the country— we lived on a farm but we didn't farm the land—and spending a great deal of time with my neighbors. My father was not around a lot, and [I] really adopted the neighbor farmer as a surrogate father in a sense, and learned a lot about hard farm work and lots of other lessons in life during those years, [from] third grade to seventh grade.

I am the child of an alcoholic father, and his immersion in business and the pressures thereof moved his drinking along during these same years. He was under tremendous pressure when we were living out in the country, and that's part of the reason I didn't see a lot of him. We always—as a family, in terms of the kids—put pressure on for him to get out of business altogether. We knew there was some dysfunction, but we didn't know why. We knew he drank too much, and we were aware that he would lose control on many occasions. But it wasn't until my junior high years that things became a little more severe.

My own drinking took place probably in late junior high— maybe tenth grade in high school. Among my friends, drinking was a fashionable thing to experiment with. Going out on the golf course and drinking wine or beer, I guess, was my introduction to drinking. I remember one of the first occurrences was sneaking into a university bar and throwing up in the bathroom, as a rude introduction to the drinking program.

The family situation deteriorated in the summer between high school and college. My mother separated from my dad, and that came as quite a rude awakening to me. We were pretty well protected from any troubles they might have had. It turns out my mother had been planning a separation for many years—seven years she had put off the inevitable in the name of her kids. Possibly questionable wisdom, but it did come as a shock to most of us, to learn that it was over.

That next year—'68 or '69—I was beginning my first year in a university. We went to a quite well-known pioneer in family therapy, the entire family, once a week, for a couple hours, for a year, and it amazes me now to think that at no time did his drinking surface as a fundamental background problem to the family's dysfunction. . . . In any case that move, from therapy into a full divorce and I out of the house, had a pretty big emotional impact on me. That's about the time I date my beginning of addiction behavior—to marijuana, my drug of choice. Ironically I smoked my first joint—a joint presented to my father as a Christmas present. I guess my parents talked it over and decided it wouldn't be a good model behavior for him to smoke it, so my sister ended up giving it to me. It was probably the most enjoyable high I ever had. December of '67. From that point I gradually became enamored of marijuana and was also very involved in the drug culture in general at that time. I started what became close to a twenty-year, or eighteen-year, addiction to that drug.

I guess I was also in a fairly rebellious mode. During this period of time I dropped out of college in the summer of '69—again, about the same time as the separation—and became very involved in political movements and Black Liberation political movements, which were intense at that time, especially at our university. I found a great degree of camaraderie and sense of family that, looking back, may have affected my interests. Drugs [were] sort of part of the game at that point. I think a lot of people involved during that time in the drug culture moved on and out of their use of drugs, beyond maybe a recreational level.

I just sort of never did move out of it. As time went on I became pretty much a daily marijuana smoker. I also took many other drugs during that period of time, and that drug use pretty well dropped away by maybe '71 or '72, but marijuana smoking stayed with me. I guess I just really loved the drug.

I moved to New York in 1971 and was there for six years, very heavily involved in political activity, involved in various groups and under lots of pressures that led to a nervous breakdown in the fall of 1977. [That] was really the reason that I ended up returning to Wisconsin and had a very difficult time. I had a psychotic reaction that certainly was drug-related, in terms of the background of the six years of marijuana and hashish use in New York, and probably somewhat depressed over that time, and fundamentally suppressing lots of emotion and what otherwise might have been a more mature accommodation to the emotions I was going through, especially the fear that was involved in some of the political activity I was in. [I] also was living in the Bronx by the end of that period, and there may have been real questionable purity to some of the marijuana I was smoking, and there may have been some PCP in some of the street drugs I was involved in. Nonetheless, I did have a psychotic episode. I was hospitalized for two weeks once, and then two weeks out, and then two weeks in again. Some medication in that second hospitalization pulled me back together, [but I] then proceeded into a depression about three or four months later that was worse than the psychosis. The psychosis was terrible for my family, [but] I had a fairly good time, actually. [However,] the depression was really terrible for me. I was very resistant to medication and became suicidal. After a few months I was still in follow-up therapy at the hospital, probably twice a week, but the therapy wasn't enough to pull me out. I finally acknowledged that fact and took medication for depression [in the] summer of '78. That worked, and I'll be forever thankful for it.

One of my greatest fears during my depression was that I might never be able to smoke marijuana again. When I did pull things back together, I went right back to my habit. . . . My drug problem failed to surface as a central issue. . . . I didn't, of course, focus on it, [being] in full denial, and neither did the medical staff I worked with.

So, I pulled out of the depression; continued with my career; met my current wife in 1980; moved to another town; got a good job; and generally pulled things together in good fashion, but [I] continued my daily habit. . . . In 1985 in the midst of our own couples' marriage counseling, our therapist centered on my marijuana smoking. I first brought it up in one session, and then the following session she really focused in on it and asked me to be evaluated. Upon being evaluated I had no trouble realizing that I was addicted, because the evidence was pretty long and heavy that I couldn't control that behavior after some eighteen years. The evaluation suggested that I quit, which I did. I was in a very low-level outpatient program at a hospital, and they put me into an AA regime, which I was quite resistant to, although [I] accommodated their wishes. Within a couple [of] months I was also involved in weekly group therapy, and [I] started to see some good changes in my life. [I] continued to attend AA meetings. In the first two years I was going to four or five meetings a week, and then probably dropping down to a couple meetings a week in the second or third years.

    . . . But I was always withholding part of myself, from the first meeting to the last. My dad is, was, and remains an atheist, my mother an agnostic. Growing up Unitarian—a very liberal and open religion—[AA's] kind of doctrinaire attitude and foundation of God-related program, I didn't take to. I realized the value of meetings and the camaraderie and the group, and I will always be indebted to AA for those portions of the program, because I think it really did pull me through, and I did successfully recover. But I never felt totally accepted within any of the meetings, because I just didn't believe in God or a higher power, and there was no way I was going to. I did everything I could to accommodate them in terms of calling the group the higher power, and anything else I could think of. Anytime I addressed my mis-givings I felt a deathly silence descend on the meeting. I never could get into any kind of intellectual dialogue with anyone; it was always clichéd responses that many of us are well aware of. . . .

In any case, I, in concert with a fellow Unitarian at our church, began looking and actually came across something about SOS—right at the same time another fellow in our church that I didn't know was doing so. We decided to begin a meeting in our church. . . . We had our first meeting January 12, 1989. . . . The nature of the group and the discussion contrast incredibly with your typical AA meeting. And it's important to me and has been important in the recovery of many other people, including several who have never known any kind of recovery program, and I think that's the most interesting thing about the evolution of SOS—its effect on people that are in early recovery and trying to pull themselves together and are exposed to it before ever getting immersed in AA at all. So I think those are interesting folks to talk to. . . .

Sam: Thanks for your interesting insights, Eric. Doug?

Doug: I'm Doug, 49 years old, and sober a little more than nine years. I was born in Michigan in 1942. My father was an alcoholic. At a very early age I was adopted by my mother's brother, an alcoholic. My adopted mother drank, but she stopped drinking shortly after they took me in. I was an only child. . . .

My father hated my natural father, and every time he looked at me, he'd think of my natural father. The resentment was always there, there was never any close—. He went out of his way to make life as miserable as he could for me. As an alcoholic, every once and a while he'd be nice, and then the following day or the middle of it, turn. There was no constant there. Every time I'd think that we could become close, he'd pull away and do the opposite. He established friendships with people my age—other kids—and to them he was a really nice person. Finally I came to accept that we could never become close. That really stopped being a problem for me once I accepted it and dealt with it at that level, at a realistic level.

Every function that my family went to, there was always drinking. The earliest drinking I can remember, I filled a beer bottle with water and went around pretending like I was drunk. Everybody accepted the fact that I was pretending. Then I got the real beer and proceeded to get drunk. It was [when I was] real young. I don't know exactly, but it was quite young.

It wasn't until I was, oh, 16 I think, that me and my cousin used to go to the grocery store and steal wine, and then we'd go to the movies, to the drive-in theaters. I used to think that we had a really great bunch of friends because we all took the same chance stealing the wine, but after I drank all mine, they offered me theirs too. I had total blackouts. I had terrible, terrible hangovers. I'd wake up in the morning with footprints all over me, and I found out later that they were walking on me— that was a game that they'd play when I got real drunk. That's when I found out that I had to control my drinking to a certain extent. There was no way I could drink the way I wanted to, because if I did people actually walked all over me.

As I got older my drinking progressed and got worse. Before I was 21 I was an alcoholic. I looked around at the other people in the area who were alcoholics, and it didn't seem so bad to me. Those people were characters. Nobody really messed around with them. They had respect. They had excitement in their life.

I really didn't see anything that wrong with being an alcoholic. I continued to have blackouts. I got in trouble with the law for stealing to get alcohol. When I became 21, I drank all the time. I'd drive home, and I'd wake up in the morning and have a bottle of beer and a shot of whiskey. I'd go out and see if my car was still there and then walk around it and see if there was dents. We lived in a small community, so the police would pull me over [when] I was too drunk to even walk, but they'd let me drive home, because people knew each other there. If it wasn't for that, I'd have been arrested for DWI.

I married and we had a daughter, and my drinking slacked off some when I married, because I could only drink on the weekends. Still, though, I tried to have a beer every morning when I woke up. My wife thought that she could change my drinking, [but] I raised a daughter with the same type of thing that my father had done to me—there was no constant: one minute I'd be a nice guy, the next minute I'd be rotten. I really did not know how to be a father. My wife helped me quite a bit, but the drinking still interfered with it. It wasn't until [my daughter] was grown up when I stopped drinking and tried to establish a closer relationship with her. Now, we got a very close relationship, and somehow, she doesn't really blame me that much for the way that she was raised, she doesn't hold a lot of anger toward me. With her effort and my wife's they finally told me that if I didn't go into a treatment, they'd leave.

It had gotten to the point where my wife was hoping that I'd get in an accident and kill myself—that way she wouldn't have to deal with it. Toward the last part of my drinking I was self-employed, so I could drink every day. And I drank, usually, about a case to two cases of beer in the daytime, and I carried a half-pint of schnapps with me all the time and used that as a breath freshener. My big concern was if I woke up in the morning and I had my couple of beers and my shots and went out, I was afraid I'd get stopped first thing in the morning and get a DWI. There was no time during the day that I'd have passed a blood test if they had given me one. I went into a treatment program to get my wife and my daughter off my back, to give me a break. My body was feeling the effects of the years of drinking.

For the first two weeks of recovery, life was like a haze. Two weeks into the treatment was the first time I had been sober in a long, long time. That's when I decided to give it a try, to see if I could even survive in the world sober. I learned that our emotional growth stops when we drink, and that's what I felt like. I felt like I was a little boy in a 40-year-old man's body. And I had to survive in the world where people expected me to act like a man, and I really wasn't—I was a little kid. And I made a commitment to try, no matter what happened, because if I lost my business, if I lost my wife, if I lost all my friends, and if I ended up on skid row, I was going to give it all I had to live a life sober, to see if I could even survive.

I think that's what kept me sober those years was that total commitment that no matter what happens in my life, I wasn't going to drink. I'd become very close to my wife. My wife explains it, like it was bringing a stranger into the house, it was like we were starting all over again. We built a happy life together. A lot of times I'll wake up in the morning, and my wife will be there, and we'll hug, tell each other we love each other. My daughter will call and she'll tell us that she loves us. My dog is there wagging her tail, and we got a cat that jumps on us and wants love. It's starting a day with all a person could ever ask for.

Before I went into the hospital program, my wife had checked several times with AA, to see if they could help. The first time that she checked, they told her just to leave the son of a bitch, and that was their advice. The next time, we arranged a meeting with one of the members outside of the club, where he would talk to me. I talked with him, I explained to him a little about my beliefs, that I didn't use prayer in my life. He said that I had to pray, and I had to accept a higher power, or else I couldn't get sober. And he wasn't even going to let me come to a meeting unless I acknowledged prayer, a higher power, and that a higher power would save me. I couldn't accept what he was saying. Finally, he decided to let me into a meeting, and I went to a speaker meeting. The speaker said the only way a person can stay sober is by accepting God, by praying. So I decided that if this was the only way, I was going to continue to be a drunk. This wasn't for me.

So about a year went by before I went into a hospital. When I went into the hospital I told them of my experience with AA, and that if they didn't have anything to offer me except prayer, then I was wasting my time and their time. The hospital said, "No, they would be giving me information, and they'd be doing workshops and things, and teaching me how to stay sober and learning about the disease of alcoholism, but AA was still mandatory." I went. I didn't like what was being said at AA, but people in the hospital supported me, and they told me to ignore a part of it, to find something at a meeting that was beneficial. I kept going to meetings because these people were telling me this is what I really needed to do, [even though] the meetings were causing me pain. I was in discomfort, because these people were not accepting me. They couldn't accept that I was staying sober through my own effort. They wanted me to be like them. They told me in the hospital to go to meetings, be the first one there and the last one to leave if I wanted to be a part of the meeting, the membership. And that's what I did. I hung out at the clubs an awful lot, and I never found out until, oh, at least a year into my sobriety, that these people were meeting at a restaurant, and I was never invited there. They were civil to me, but I was never a part of the group. I was always open and honest in my discussions at the AA club, but finally the meetings caused me more pain and harm than they did good. So I stopped going for a number of years.

Then I ran across that article in *Free Inquiry*, written by James Christopher, and it was as if it was *me* that was writing it. I called and was interested in the SOS group. Before that I had met Hal, an atheist in another club. I told him about my discomfort in AA, and he said, "Well, if it becomes bad enough, we can always start a group on our own." When we realized how difficult it would be to start it, and how much work would have to be put into it, we just both put it aside, and hoped that someday someone else would come forward with enough determination to put the work into it, to follow it through. That's why I was so glad to see what SOS was doing. The philosophy of SOS, I'm in total agreement with; that there's no other way for everyone, that we're all individuals, and that a higher power may work for some people, but others need a rational approach. *I* did it myself, through my own efforts. It wasn't due to a higher power, and the group only helped me to a certain extent, but the rest of it was me that did it. And I accepted the responsibility for my success or failure. SOS . . . is the best-kept secret in recovery that there is.

When Rational Recovery (RR) first started, I was on a radio show talking about SOS, and a caller called in and asked me if I was familiar with RR, and I wasn't at that time. . . . One of the counselors that I was in treatment with mentioned RR, and I asked her for their number. She said a Dr. _____ was in charge of the RR group. I called [him] to find out a little bit about RR, and we talked over the phone. It sounded like we really had a lot in common. And the idea came across that our two groups could intermingle—we could go to each other's meetings. The people from our meeting went to talk to Dr. _____ and one of the people there. [The doctor] got out the blackboard and did his thing on what we had to do to stay sober, and the people in [our] group wanted nothing to do with [it]. They said that they would never go to another meeting again. I wanted to give him a second chance, to see if he wouldn't be quite so rigid in what he was saying. The thing about the anniversaries—the celebration of sobriety—he thought that was wrong. Calling ourselves an alcoholic he thought was wrong. If a person isn't drinking, then they don't have a problem and they can't be an alcoholic. They can only be an alcoholic while they're actively drinking, according to him.

According to him, the problem isn't with the alcohol or the physical addiction, it's with the way a person thinks. By listening to him and doing what he tells you, [you'll learn] how to think properly. And you can continue to drink while you're coming to the meetings; just change the way that you're thinking, and the sobriety will automatically follow. His idea of continued sobriety isn't enforced. If a person has a slip or takes a drug, there isn't any problem if that person doesn't have a major disaster in their life, if they don't go out and wreck their car or if they don't do any harm to someone. If it's a harmless drunk or a harmless drug bout, then they shouldn't consider it as a slip. What they celebrate is how many months or years they don't have a problem with alcohol or drugs. By not having a problem with it, doesn't mean that you are abstinent—it just means that you didn't get a DWI, or you didn't kill somebody, or something, that particular year, or week, or whatever. I couldn't agree with that at all. I think total abstinence is so important for me—I just couldn't do it any other way. And I think it's dangerous, his philosophy.

I told him that I didn't use alcohol mouthwash, I used a herbal mouthwash. He said anyone who didn't use mouthwash— alcoholic mouthwash—was a fanatic. And I told him that for me to take alcohol, and swish it around in my mouth, and spit it out, was just ridiculous. It was just too dangerous. And even if I didn't swallow it, for me, I'd be afraid that enough of the alcohol would enter my system to trigger a physical response. There's no reason to use alcohol when there's other alternatives out there. I know of people in AA who use alcohol mouthwashes, and if they're able to, that's fine; but for me, it wasn't an option. Because of my stance, he thought I was some type of fanatic, and he told me that I couldn't stay sober the way I was doing things, that I'd have to get drunk.

He was in absolute control of the group. Someone supposedly ran the group while he wasn't there, but that person was like a miniature Dr. _____. As soon as they could learn all the responses that [the doctor] would give and could quote him word for word, then he'd let them go out on their own. It was a robot program, where you go in, and you come out as a Dr. _____ clone. There was no compromise. There was only one way to do it, and that was it. For someone who's unable to think, if they were in really bad shape, . . . it's extremely difficult to argue with a psychiatrist who's trained in that area.

We also came up with the question of "hypothetically, how

much I could drink before it triggered a physical response?" According to him I could drink a quarter of a beer and it wouldn't cause me any problem. He said I could probably drink a half a beer, or even a whole beer. He said I'd probably get in trouble on my second or third beer, but he said for me to have a half a beer or a beer shouldn't really be a problem. According to him, alcoholism is a thinking problem, and he completely ignores the physical problem.

I think heredity plays a big, big part in it. When I was young drinking, for me, was such a good feeling, I couldn't understand why anyone would want not to drink, or why anyone would want to stop drinking. When I was young, . . . I couldn't understand why they would not drink during the day. I believe that my body processes it different from other people, and it really doesn't matter if I'm right or not, but because I believe that, I can't take a drink. If that's true, that means that it's a physical problem, and it has nothing to do with my spiritual life, and it has to be dealt with as a physical problem. And the way to deal with it is to take it completely out of my life. . . .

Sam: Thank you for concisely restating the Sobriety Priority for us, Doug.

Louise, you look eager to participate. Louise?

Louise: I'm Louise, one year, five months sober, 35 years old. I'm married. I was born in New York, but I've lived in Florida since 1967. . . . My mother, my father, my stepmother, my sister, all live here. My other sister died when she was 23. My younger brother is 33, and he lives in California.

My father hasn't had a drink in about a year, from what I understand, but he drank heavily the whole time I was growing up. My older sister drank and was a heroin addict. She recovered from heroin addiction, so to speak, about two years before she died, but she was drunk when she died. She drowned. My sister who's still living also has a drinking problem. She had a baby a year ago, and seems to have subsided a bit, although I wouldn't say she's experiencing any kind of recovery. She's experiencing a drop off in the amount of liquor consumption, just because of her work and because she has a baby to take care of.

We lived on Long Island, New York, when I was a kid because my dad had been transferred to New York City. He was with the FBI and he commuted into the city every day. We lived in a working-class neighborhood. My dad usually was gone on a train by the time we got up, and he didn't come home until after we went to bed. I didn't see that much of him; at least I don't remember him that much. I do remember that we were to just "watch out." Don't hassle him. Don't bug him. Don't speak to him unless he speaks to you. Just stay out of his way or you will be real sorry.

My mom was a long-suffering, I'm-doing-this-for-my-children type gal. Maybe she has a glass of wine every now and then, but she doesn't have any kind of substance abuse problem or drinking problem. She's just a my-whole-life-is-my-family–type, despite her bachelor's degree in music education. While my dad was still on a supply ship in the South Pacific, she stayed home, raised her kids. That's the way it was supposed to be.

My mother was, and is still, very devout. We always went to the Methodist Church every Sunday, and went to Sunday School, and all that kind of stuff. My dad went, too, although probably in about 1964 or 1965, when the Civil Rights movement was really getting into full swing, he stopped attending because, of course, all this love and brotherhood stuff was kind of subversive, and he didn't really want to be involved in it. . . .

We moved to Florida when I was 11. We had lived in a blue-collar neighborhood, but when we moved I don't know what happened. Maybe my father got a massive raise. He bought a four-bedroom waterfront home and a new car. But our family life just got worse and worse, because Dad was drinking. From the minute he came in from work at about five-thirty, you didn't talk to him until he had his two martinis. Period. You didn't even look at him if you could possibly avoid it.

About the time Nixon was president my sister was using drugs and was really involved in anti–Vietnam activities. My dad was always having to write letters to Washington to explain why his daughter was on the front page of the newspaper carrying a sign that said "Nixon Go Home." About this time I was starting to get the drift that even though I was "good" and I was staying out of trouble with the folks, and my sisters were "bad" and were doing all this stuff they weren't supposed to do, they were having fun and I wasn't. So I decided that now it was *my* turn. I started to smoke pot [when] I was between 13 and 14.

About that time they sent me to a psychiatrist. I was just starting to act up. Both my sisters had been under a psychiatrist's care for years, for all the good it did. So I guess my parents just panicked, "Oh, my God, she's starting to act like a human being! Quick! Get her to the shrink!" This guy was just giving me every kind of sedative and tranquilizer that you could ask for. I would only take my prescribed medication to purposely OD, to try and kill myself—which I attempted eight times within about three years as a teenager. Then I'd wake up in the hospital, and I'd say, "Oh God! I'm still here! Damn, I can't do anything right."

My psychiatrist told my parents that it would be best for me if they split up because being around my father was not good for me at all. He really had to leave. So my mom had him served with a court order to vacate while he was at work—in the Federal Building. He had no clue. Real good, Mom! About the time this thing was going to be delivered, she and my sister—who were the only ones home besides me—split. "We're going to go shopping. See ya!" They're out the door. And my dad comes home, and he's crying. I'd never seen him cry in my life, and I'm sitting there on the couch. "What's going on? What's the matter?" And he said, "Well, Dr. So-and-so said it's best for you if I don't live here anymore. So I'm leaving." My dad packed a suitcase and out he went. The guilt—it was just horrible.

I was pretty much doing as I damn well pleased for the next couple of years, which boiled down to just doing drugs, a *lot* of drugs. I drank every now and then, but at the time it didn't really seem to make that much sense to drink; for one thing you could get high a lot faster with drugs. And at the time it was a lot cheaper to get drugs than it was to drink, and drugs were more readily available.

I used anything I could get my hands on. I tripped probably 350 times, back when you could still get acid and mescaline. One of the easiest ways to get drugs—and the cheapest, or so I thought —was to have sex with older guys. You could get anything you wanted. I had absolutely no problem with that. I didn't like it, but it was a means to an end. I wasn't really into stealing: for some reason my conscience would never let me steal. Maybe it was a bit of my dad's influence. That was one of the main ways that my girlfriends and I had for getting drugs. You want to get high? Get out on the road, stick out your thumb, and see what comes along. We did that every weekend for years. . . .

About the time I turned 18, I started drinking. It's funny, because I can't ever remember taking a drink until I was of the legal age to do so, but I was doing every kind of dope you can imagine up until then. Gradually I drank a little more, I drugged a little less; I drank a little more, I drugged a little less. I quit doing what we used to call "chemicals" when I was about 22 or 23. That's when I really started to drink—*a lot.* I don't ever remember drinking like other people. At first I didn't drink every day or even every weekend, . . . but when I drank, I drank to extreme intoxication. And I would always, *always,* end up (a) trying to convince somebody to go home with me, (b) not having to try too hard at all to convince somebody to go home with me, or (c) making a big tearful scene in a public place because no one would go home with me. Needless to say, it was pretty weird.

I did that for several years, and then I met my first husband. I was drunk at a bar when I met him. What a surprise! He did not have a drinking problem. He was a super nice guy who thought I was tourist. . . . Six weeks after I moved in with Larry, I was drinking one night, got upset about something that happened with my nephew, and I decided that the best thing to do to relax me was to get in my car and take a drive. So I drove to the nearest bar, drank a little bit more, and got back in the car and drove some more. I ended up doing a DWI. The way that the cops found out was that somebody who was in all probability even more drunk than I was crossed the center line in his four-wheel-drive truck and hit me head on at forty miles an hour. While I was bleeding to death in the emergency room, somebody got a little sample and decided that "Yup, yup, she's drunk, too." That was the worst thing that ever happened to me in my life. . . . Tore my nose almost completely off my face. Broke all my ribs on my right side. Broke my collar bone. I had 250 stitches in my face and the side of my head. It was a real drag, to say the least. But it didn't connect. It never crossed my mind that "Gee, maybe I shouldn't have drunk and gotten in my car and driven." The guy that hit me was so drunk that he stood in the road and told the cop that I had crossed the center line and hit him—except that he was in the wrong lane and my car was off the side of the road and had the driver's side torn off of it. It just didn't connect. I didn't feel that I had done anything wrong. It's kind of a shame that I didn't, because I wonder sometimes that if the circumstances had been a little different, maybe I would have given in to the fact that there was a problem. But there were some witnesses following along behind me, who saw this take place and testified that I was going the speed limit, that I wasn't weaving or anything like that. . . .

Since my then-boyfriend was kind enough not to toss me out for being a jerk or Bride-of-Frankenstein–looking for almost a year, I decided that the thing to do would be to repay him with my life. So I got married to him. He still didn't drink much —maybe a beer on Saturday. I smoked pot every day of my life at the time. Not a lot. I had a little bitty pipe and I just had my little bowl of pot when I came home from work.

After a couple of years things had started to get real boring. For one thing he wouldn't drink with me. He didn't want to do anything—which to me was to go out and drink, stay home and drink, or go to somebody's house and drink. He didn't want to have fun. He wanted to do boring stuff like woodworking, and making boats; and reading about furniture design. My God! "This guy is a bore and a half," I thought. "I have to get out of here somehow." . . .

So I got divorced. I started doing some really weird shit when I was drinking. I got to the point where I would go to places where I knew that dangerous people hung out. There used to be several bars on the beach where commercial fishermen hung out. These guys are some bad dudes. One bar was named Mel's. We'd call it Mel's Knife and Gun Club. Everybody in there had a weapon of some sort, and people were always getting stabbed. That's the kind of place I wanted. "Let-me-at-'em! I'm going for the gusto here." . . .

I'd go to these places and zero in on the most dangerous-looking person there. At the time I had a really nice apartment. I was doing well financially. I had a lawsuit settlement in the bank in the glory days when CDs were $13\frac{1}{4}$ percent. I envisioned myself as sort of an Isadora Duncan–type. I thought I was terribly, terribly glamorous. I lived in this beautiful place with arched windows—*arched windows*—and had money to spare. My pride and joy was the fact that I'd had all these top-shelf liquors at home in case anyone dropped by, things that I didn't even drink. I never cared for whiskey or Jack Daniels or bourbon, but I always had it at home. And I always had beer. It wasn't all horrible and degrading, but it just seemed like it got worse and worse. Every-thing became secondary to getting high. And I could really drink a lot. I could drink a lot and no one would even know that I'd been drinking. There's a school of thought that says you *think* that they didn't know. I *guarantee* it. People did not know. I think I learned a lot about lying and wearing the perfect face for being high and drunk from being around my father. If he knew you were high, you were dead. . . .

It's funny how you get to be a creature of habit. I'd get

off of work Friday and go home and take an hour's nap so I could stay up late. I would get dressed, go out, and I would eat my dinner at an Irish place, a bar—not completely a bar, but as the night gets later and later there's fewer people eating and a lot more people drinking. I'd get some dinner, have a couple of drinks. From there I would go to a place that was quite a drive, but I liked it. And the people there, I always felt, were all Lynyrd Skynyrd–type fans, or not quite country and western but not really New Wave. I'd go up there and everybody thought I was a little creepy. I wouldn't do anything; I wouldn't say anything. People just ate that shit up—especially coming from a gal, especially coming from a gal who obviously had money to spend. It was sort of a hippie-type place, but I was definitely into punk and New Wave, always wore black clothes, black fishnet stockings, and tons of black eye makeup, black lipstick, and black nail polish. People just went berserk when I walked in, but not in a mean way. . . .

At this point I was really drinking like crazy, having real bad blackouts, and missing work—bad, because to me it had always been, "Well, as long as I don't miss any work I'm all right," because work was the most important thing. Getting up and going to work was everything. I started to miss work, especially on—surprise—Monday. I just couldn't let the weekend stop on Saturday night. I had to get blasted Sunday night, too, and then try and drag in for Monday. I was just waiting around to die. That's when I started trying to look for somebody that seemed real dangerous, because I thought that I'm really too much of a coward to snuff my own self. Maybe I can find someone to do it for me. And I almost did, a couple of times, but the worst that they did was beat me up and take all my money in the privacy of my own boudoir. So I just was hanging out at this place, . . . stayed there, got drunk, and said nothing to anyone. I just sat there and waited for Mr. Death to walk in.

By this time I bought a house. (Don't let anyone tell you that you can't do anything while you're drinking, because you *can* do *some* things.) One guy was showing up at my house at all hours of the day and night, and I was afraid that my neighbors were going to start being bothered by this guy shrieking in my yard at three o'clock in the morning. I didn't hear from him for a while and then I didn't see him. But I did meet someone whom I approved of—another big drinker. . . .

We drank together for the first couple of years we knew each other, and drank real, real heavily, although he started to taper off a long time before it occurred to me that it might be a problem. I'd go to his apartment, spend the night, and I'd want to get home so that I could have a drink—and this was ten o'clock Saturday morning. And I'd always have an excuse: I've got to feed my cats, I've got to get home, whatever reason. By the time I'd get home I'd have only one drink. I was very drink specific: Black Russians—three ounces of vodka, one ounce of Kahlua, two ice cubes. I could prepare it in my sleep. I didn't get really trashed —I wouldn't drink five or six of them before noon—but I would stay buzzed the whole weekend and get smashed. We'd go to different places and do different things. I really don't even know what made him think that maybe he ought to not drink so much or to think it's a problem, although we argued a lot when we had both been drinking heavily. We used to get into some really nasty arguments—no punches pulled and no holds barred. Real nasty stuff. And while he was drinking less and less, I think I was probably drinking more and more and getting those same feelings again: "Oh, God, here's another pantywaist! This guy just doesn't know how to have fun, that's the problem with him." It got to the point where I was absolutely trashed every night. I was devastatingly hung over every morning. I was starting to have trouble functioning at work.

My manager knew that something was wrong. My company has a "wellness" program with free psychological counseling. I'd go in to a psychologist who said, "Well, of course you're drinking too much. You're depressed." And I thought, "Damn, I knew that was it. I knew I was right! I knew I was right! So once I

don't get depressed any more then I'll just naturally cut down."
Well, it didn't happen. And what's more, I got more and more
depressed. And then my boyfriend started to say, "No, let's not
have another drink. Let's do something else." He didn't really bug
me or pester me about drinking, though. I don't really think he
gave me an ultimatum, but finally it just got to the point where
I knew if something didn't give (a) I was going to be alone again,
and (b) I was without question to die. I knew I was. I couldn't
function without my Black Russians, but I couldn't function with
them either. It's the old adage that you can't get sober but you
can't get drunk either. There was absolutely nothing fun about it
anymore, nothing festive: just constant maintenance drinking. So
I did something that even now I kind of think is a somewhat radical concept, because I haven't yet talked to anybody else that has
done this. I knew that I was probably an alcoholic. I knew that
all along. Anybody who can read English knows that it runs in
families, and my Dad has definitely got a problem, and so does
everybody else except my mother and my brother. It's a disease.
We've all got it. What do you do when you get a disease? Go
to the doctor.

I went to the doctor and said, "I have tried to stop drinking
and I can't. Last week I did the ceremonial dumping down the
sink of the booze and said I'm never going to drink again! That's
it! No more! Right now until forever! It lasted about two hours.
That's when I really got scared. Shit, I can't even go two hours?
This is insane. I can't live like this anymore." . . .

She asked, "Do you think you can go from now until bed-
time without taking a drink?"

"I guess I could."

"I'll tell you what, when you really do this, you're not going
to be feeling so good some days. I really don't think that you
need to go to an inpatient detox, but you're going to have a
rough weekend. I'm going to give you a prescription for Valium.
Take them exactly as you are instructed to, because you're not
getting any more. Know that: from this moment on, this is it;

you're not getting any more. Secondly, I'm going to write you another prescription, for Antabuse. Get up tomorrow, take one, and, whatever you do, don't drink once you take that Antabuse, because either you will come so close to dying that you will wish you were dead or you will just be so sick that you're going to have to be hospitalized. It will put you in a real hurting way." So that's what I did. Unfortunately, for the next year and a half I would go three months without drinking, and then I would drink. Another three months, and then I would drink. . . .

I had to come up with some actual, solid concrete things that I personally was going to do to keep myself from drinking. One of them, of course, was counseling. I started lifting weights. I started riding a bicycle. And I was such a klutz when I was a kid! I was one of those kids that wore big, thick glasses and made straight As and was afraid of the hall. But now, I'm thirty-five years old! And I'm an athlete! I never thought it would have happened. Bad things feed off of bad things, like depression and alcoholism. The good things feed off of the good things. If I stay physically fit because it helps me not to drink, and I don't drink because that would not make me physically fit. I learned how to chill out. . . . And I've learned how to appreciate mundane things, like watching TV, or taking a bike ride, or going to the beach.

I have remarried. It's been great being married to somebody who's not only a wonderful guy whom I love very dearly, but it's helped me a lot just being around him and being married to a sober person. I don't know what people do with spouses who drink socially. I don't think I could handle that. I don't know if I'll ever feel comfortable with drinking alcohol again. Because of my history of relapse I'd prefer not to test it. Joe goes to concerts and nightclubs and places where they serve alcohol and it doesn't bother him a bit, but it bothers me a lot and I don't do it. Last time I went to a place that served alcohol, I drank it. And the last time I drank, I drank at the bar. I want to go into those places. People will say I should be able to get over that or grow out of it or recover sufficiently to be able to go into these places. Why? Why would I want to? Sure, Joe does. If it doesn't bother him, that's fine. I'm glad that he can. I can't and I'm not going to try to force myself just to give this bullshit happy couple impression. We're a happy couple with him going this way and me going that. We have our own lives too. I'm not, at least at last look, sutured to him in any way, so what the heck? Joe and I are both active in SOS, although we sometimes prefer to attend meetings separate from each other.

It's getting toward a year and five months since I've had a drink. I never thought I'd go this long. You have to find your own way. SOS recognizes that. I don't have to buy into everything that one organization or another espouses. To me it's more of interest to be in a room full of other people not drinking.

Sam: It *is* amazing what we can do with some nonjudgmental support. Thanks, Louise.
Kenneth?

Kenneth: I'm Kenneth, I'm 51, and my dry date is Christmas 1976 —I've been sober for sixteen years. I was born in Massachusetts, in a suburb of Boston. At an early age my parents moved about twenty miles out from Boston. It was a really nice little town— rural, woods. I had, as best I can recollect, a very happy childhood. I was the youngest. My mother had me when she was 40 years old. . . . All the attention was focused on me. I guess I wasn't a bad kid, and I don't remember anything really traumatic.

My father quit drinking when I was about 5, and so he was sober. Nothing in my past would indicate that I should have a need and have a problem with drinking. When I first drank alcohol I was probably 14 years old, and I hated the taste of the stuff— hated the smell of it, the taste of it, didn't like anything. But once I had managed to choke down three cans of beer, I really liked the effect, and I was one of these people who drank for effect. Because I looked very young, didn't have a fake ID, and the drinking age in Florida was 21 at the time, I didn't have a lot of opportunities to drink. Somebody else would have to buy the beer for me, usually a couple of guys.

I didn't really start drinking until I was in the Navy and stationed in California, and we could drink on the base. The beer hall (the Marines call it a Slop Shoot), was in the Marine barracks, which was just across the street from the Navy barracks, and I left the Slop Shoot and walked across the street to the Navy barracks, and went to bed. That was it. You couldn't get in any trouble, really. Even then I don't remember it being a problem. At that time in the military service, you really had to get seriously out of line with drinking for them to consider it a problem. It was kind of the natural thing for a sailor to do, drink, when he was not on duty.

My first recollection of a real problem was after two years of being in California. I was transferred to Midway Island—twelve hundred miles from Hawaii and a pretty miserable place. There was plenty of booze to drink, and very cheap—fifteen to twenty cents for a beer or something. You were almost encouraged to drink, although most people didn't. I certainly did, and I thought, "Oh, this is the one thing I can do out here. I can drink this mess away." I had my first blackout there. I went to bed, in my bunk, took off my clothes, put them in my locker, and couple of hours later I woke up in the empty half of the barracks, sleeping on some bare springs and soaking wet. Don't know how I got wet. And I remember sneaking back to—they call it the "cube," because they had lockers arranged in a cube for four people to sleep—sneaking back in there and hoping nobody saw me. I was saying, "Boy, they're going to think I'm nuts," because I had no idea how I got to that other end of the barracks. And I never told them. Nobody saw me. But I thought, "This is some kind of a sign. You're starting to crack up." I made no connection that it was the alcohol I consumed. I just thought it was a sign of some sort of mental instability.

My father got cancer, and I was pulled off that island and sent back home, because it was terminal. I was stationed here for a couple of months and drank pretty heavily but was able to report for duty every day. In fact I was commended [for service] under the stress of my father's death; the commanding officer gave me a letter. The way I handled it was I'd drink every night.

After I got out of the service, I spent a period in New York at a shipping dry dock in New York City, Brooklyn Navy Yard, and I liked going to Greenwich Village to drink there. Nobody on the ships would go with me, because they didn't like going to places where all those homosexuals and strange people were. So I usually went alone, and you would think I would have had a problem, but the only thing that really happened to me that I remember was that I had my wallet lifted twice, and falling asleep in the subway of all places. I can remember when the ship pulled out of there, I says, "Thank God we're leaving New York City, because if I stayed there I'd be an alcoholic."

Later on I had a job, after I got out of the service, working with DDT for the State Board of Health. They were trying to eradicate the yellow fever mosquito. I sprayed pesticides for about four years with no protection. DDT. There was some doubt, when I started having problems, what was the actual cause, whether I was being poisoned by the DDT or the alcohol. I started having problems, like wanting to steer my car off the bridge when I was driving across, and shakes, and the typical fear of the unknown, the fear of police. But it was just a whole lot of the nervous conditions and I really started to come unglued. I finally ended up going to AA.

[This was] probably [when I was] about 29. After a couple of false starts, I think I finally got about a year and a half of sobriety under my belt. Things weren't too bad. I had the attitude about AA at that time that I don't have any choice; this is the only game in town; I've got to make it work. I didn't really like a lot of stuff that was going on—some of their philosophy— and still take issue with the idea that some people are incapable of being honest with themselves. It's like AA never fails; it's always the person that's coming in that failed.

I stayed sober for about a year and a half; however, at that time it was really taboo to talk about drugs of any kind. Marijuana was never discussed. And I had smoked marijuana maybe once or twice in New York City, smoked it and got high. I liked the effect. At the time drinking was more important and more readily available. But when I met a woman—at a singles dance I think it was—who was not in AA, or not sober, and she used to tell me, she says, "I've got this marijuana, and I don't know how to smoke it." And I thought, "Boy, this is it! So, I'm going to have sex with this woman, and I'm going to get high, and we're going to have a great time." That's exactly what happened. And you couldn't have gotten me away from that stuff after that.

It didn't make much sense after a while. I was able to get high smoking pot. Didn't give a damn about drinking. In fact the mood back in that period, probably 1968, was alcoholics were called "juice freaks," and it was really in and cool to smoke dope. You were naturally superior and into Peace and Love; juice freaks like to fight and redneck. For anybody who hadn't lived in that period or experienced some of those things, it was hard to believe some of the misconceptions and how naive we were about a lot of things. But pot was considered a good drug—couldn't possibly hurt you. All that negative stuff about it was lies made up by the government for some unknown reason. I felt the more I attended AA meetings, and the more I heard about the drinkalogues, the less I identified with being an alcoholic. Because I'd never been any of those things. The hairier their stories got, the less I could identify. I was a member of a young people's AA group. I had heard the other people in my group talk about their drinking experiences, and a lot of them were pretty bad. I really did not have [bad things happen]—I rolled a Volkswagen and had a sprained wrist out of the deal, and the insurance paid for all the damage, and I was not charged with drinking. I lost a girlfriend. But anything really serious, at that time the cops would nod and wink, too. There was a time when I smashed a car in between two parked trucks and got charged with "public intoxication and careless driving," which now would be go right from here to jail. But at that time they were trying to cut you some slack.

So I left the area in pursuit of a girlfriend I met in upstate New York, and when we decided we were going to California, we got as far as Milwaukee and ran out of money. So I made an AA connection there, and this time the AA connection was with young people in AA who smoked dope and stayed sober. And I thought, "This is pretty good. This is not like at home. These guys are cool and they know what's happening." So I went to AA meetings up there and smoked pot. When I left Milwaukee and went to Los Angeles, I stopped going to AA altogether. I think maybe I've tried one meeting.

I got involved with some people—a Catholic Worker group —and they were feeding bums on Skid Row, east LA. I remember there was one guy who broke just about all traditions. He was from AA and he would go down there and try to harangue and proselytize and really bother these people on Skid Row. I thought, "What a jerk! This guy has no idea what AA's about. You don't do that! You don't go into bars, or you don't go after people." Basically I was smoking pot, so there didn't seem to be any reason to be associated with AA. Watching this guy's behavior was just one more bean on the scale that I don't really need AA. Upon returning from the Los Angeles area back to Florida, I didn't go to any more meetings. I smoked dope; I did not drink.

The first crisis to come along was a girlfriend, an ex-nun whom I met out there, leaving when she didn't like my going out to bars with the guys. I was not drinking, but I was going out to the bars. She knew what was behind it—I was looking for women. She said, "If you do that tonight, . . ." Some guys came by that I knew from the bars, and she knew that tonight I'm leaving. I thought she was full of crap. She didn't have the money to go back, doesn't have a car, but'll make the trip. True to her word she was gone within a week, and then I had my reason. I say,"You know, I don't think I could be an alcoholic. I've done a little. I've done orange sunshine LSD a couple of times. Did mescaline. Smoked some black afghan hashish. I didn't go crazy. I don't do all that weird stuff I heard those people talking about in those AA meetings. So I don't think I'm an alcoholic. Well, there's only one way to prove this. Let's march down to the bar here and tie one on and see what happens." So I did. I'm only about a half a block from the bar, and drinking straight shots with beer, got pretty tight, and walked home the half a block, fell into bed, and—"See there! Nothing happened!"

I was off and running for four years maybe, maybe five. It was drinking and smoking dope. The second time I sobered up I was more or less like some of the classic stories I had heard in the AA program. I didn't have anything left. I had a suitcase full of clothes. I was in really good physical health. I was doing commercial fishing at the time with a guy. I was eating good and getting plenty of exercise and sunshine. I was in great health, but I knew mentally I was headed for the cracker factory. And it was getting worse.

Reality was becoming more and more blurred. What was possible, and what was highly improbable were almost impossible for me to separate. My rationale for drinking was that I was not an alcoholic. I was crazy. Nowhere did I see written that crazy people could not drink. Alcoholics can't drink, but crazy people, they can drink! So I was just nuts. I was content with this and would ignore the pleas of my mother and friends, anybody else who talked about my drinking. I would just dismiss it. "I'm having a great time. You've got a problem. I don't have a problem."

I woke up behind the bar one night and tried to get up and walk away. Apparently I had passed out in the dirt parking lot. I don't know what happened; maybe a car ran over me. I had a broken leg—not severe, a hairline fracture—but I could not walk. The cops let me sleep in the jail overnight until somebody could get me out to the VA hospital the next day. The VA took care of me as a Navy veteran and put a cast on my leg. When I talked to some sort of a counselor upon leaving there, I says, "I got no place to go. I've got no home. I can't work.

I've got no place to go." They couldn't give me food stamps because you can't shop with a broken leg, so they put me in a little halfway house, and that gave me a month to cool my heels. There were three meals a day. I had to be in by eleven o'clock. It was not any kind of a treatment program. To this day, I maintain this is the best a treatment program can offer: some respite from your daily routine, whatever it is, and time to reflect on what the hell's going on in your life. I didn't get any therapy.

The only therapy I got was maybe aversion therapy, because while I was there, they moved a young man in to share my room. I was about 35 and he was 28. He'd had a massive stroke, and he dragged his foot and his arm was screwed up, and his face dropped to one side, and his speech was slurred, and I knew from being in Alcoholics Anonymous that this was more than likely caused by drugs. It was a great object lesson, watching this guy. He never had any intention of stopping drinking or smoking dope. Any chance he got—. Watching him, and not having any money to go out and drink, I had a lot of time to think about where I was going, what was happening to me. As the AA meeting was probably a couple of miles away, I could either walk down on crutches or catch a bus.

As much as I hated going back to AA, I finally came to the conclusion that the only way out of this dilemma was to stop drinking, and the only way to do it was to go back to AA. So I did, and at the time I had sort of a benefactor, an older man, whom I'd known my previous time in AA. He put me up, bought me cigarettes, fed me, and was really kind to me. However, he was one of the AA fanatics. This guy lived and breathed AA. It was all he did, the focus of his whole life. He talked, lived, and breathed it. He was on the phone talking to I don't know how many newcomers every night. Curiously enough I was later to find out that this guy smoked pot and—not only that—was dealing pot within AA. He kept wanting me to go out and visit some friends of his out on the beach, "You'll really like these people. Couple of young people living right on the beach." So I went one Sunday afternoon with him, and much to my amazement somebody broke out out a bag of dope, and somebody broke out some papers, and they rolled a number, and they passed it. I didn't believe what was going on. I was stunned. It was passed to me and I smoked it. It was really a good thing, because something had happened. I just did not like the feeling. I did not like being high. I could not wait for it to wear off, and I've never had any real desire to do that again.

Some months after that, at a time when I had about eight months of being without alcohol, come Christmas, I said, "This sucks! I don't like this whole thing, this AA—. Fuck everything! I'm going—." I went back down to the bars and got drunk. It was fortuitous again: Usually nobody but alcoholics goes out to a bar on Christmas Eve, so I was there with some alcoholics. I didn't like to drink with alcoholics—they're not much fun. I didn't have any fun. I didn't like the feeling of being loaded on booze. I met a guy in the bar who gave me a ride home while he was drunk and he scared me, because his driving was really erratic. It was kind of a repeat of the same thing with pot. I says, "This is just terrible! I don't like it anymore. This is not—. These are not the people I want to be with." And I went back to the AA group the next day, and got sober, and I've been sober ever since.

It still often amazes me, when I think back of the years that I spent searching for this stuff and waiting hours to make a little marijuana deal. Something had changed in my thinking. Getting high was not just . . . I had a value on being sober. Some way it had gotten through to me somehow. The first year and maybe three or four months were probably the worst time of my life. At a recent SOS meeting we got on the subject of suicide somehow. It seemed like most of the people out there had tried or had seriously contemplated suicide, and somebody out there asked me if I had. I never have. It's hard to explain. I had almost a year's worth of a constant dialogue going on in my head, like a voice or part of my brain telling me, "This isn't worth it. You might as well kill yourself." This dialogue was about to drive me nuts. I had no desire to commit suicide. I wanted this force, this entity, whatever, that was telling me that that's what I should do, to go away and leave me alone and let me get this thing straight. It really was a tough time in my life. Being raised a Roman Catholic, with sin and redemption and punishment, and [guilt], I was really into punishing myself.

I lived a very spartan existence—nothing but TV dinners, AA meetings, and work. Very little joy in my life: a small, dingy apartment in a very low-rent area downtown and no car—walking through a bunch of panhandlers and street drunks to get to the AA meetings. To this day, I don't know how I got through it. I had a lot of support from my mother who used to write me letters after she moved to Canada; the support of the people in the fellowship.

After things gradually got better, I met some very unique people in AA. I have never considered myself to be an atheist, but I did have some problems with the religious tone of Alcoholics Anonymous. I was always kind of an odd man out as far as the rest of the fellowship was in general, but after I had some time, this didn't even bother me. An old-timer who used to be around AA would say, "it takes five to stay alive." Once I got the five years, and some of the fingerpointers, Big Book bangers, had gotten drunk in that five years, it didn't seem like I had to listen to them much anymore.

I've gotten secure enough in my sobriety that at about the ten-year mark I wasn't satisfied with the way things were and wanted something else in my life, something to give me some direction other than going off half-cocked. . . . Staying sober has gotten to be almost second nature. I haven't wanted just to stop going to meetings. I heard that story too many times. I was getting more and more uncomfortable with the meeting I was going to. Around this area most of the AA meetings seem to be more and more into the importance of the ritual and the form, the dogma;

the substance of the meeting is really secondary. It's amazing to me how short some meetings are: they will spend fifteen minutes reading the 12 Steps, 12 Traditions, the Preamble, and a couple of other things. The meeting is almost secondary: I think they really think that the substance of the meeting is in reading all this stuff. Going on vacation while I was laid off here recently gave me a break from going to that particular meeting on a Friday night. When I came back, after being gone about a month, I says, "Why go back? Just start going to SOS."

When SOS first started out, I gave them all the support I could give them. I didn't feel like it was something I wanted to get involved with, because there were a lot of people who still had a lot of pain and anger about what they perceived religion, as it exists in the United States, had done to them. . . . So I didn't really care to go, because I'm not fighting the battle of the Roman Catholic Church anymore. I had a tremendous rage and anger at it for many years. It just doesn't seem to be worth the effort anymore. But on coming back from the vacation I decided "Why not? In the times these people have met over the years, they have expended a lot of their anger also, and I don't hear as much of that as used to be going on."

One of the big problems I see for SOS is that so many of us got sober through AA. I'm sober fourteen years, and most of this has been done in AA, and naturally I have to talk about AA. This is really a dilemma. There's no way you can tell your story or your experience without talking about AA. It's no way that they're going to perceive it any other way than that you're bashing AA.

My feeling about Alcoholics Anonymous is that whatever my qualms were about it or my disagreements, I had managed to make some kind of a translation or adapt to it, and for me I really consider that it's worth a hundred precent, because I really did not expect AA to turn me into a Gandhi or a Mother Teresa. My only expectations—total sobriety, total abstinence—and I got that. So I do feel that it's worked a hundred percent.

But the agony over the years, of watching thousands and

thousands of people come through the doors of AA and not make it, and all the time the fellowship's proudly beating itself on the back and saying "How wonderful we are!" and "How we're getting bigger all the time! We're getting more and more people!" and "Isn't it wonderful!" I said, "Look, wait a minute! Don't you see what's happening? The problem seems to be getting worse out there, and you're getting more people because the problem keeps getting bigger and bigger every year. There's more and more people using drugs, more and more people abusing alcohol. I don't think it's wonderful that AA continues to grow. I think it's a sign of a major tragedy." I certainly applaud any other group— *any* other group—that can come up with some kind of solution.

I feel like Alcoholics Anonymous and the 12-step programs are now part of the problem. People who graduated or who were trained through the fellowship, the 12 Steps, are now in the institutes of mental health through all facets of the bureaucracy. It's not only infected treatment programs, it's infected government policy on how we handle it. It's allowed this government to ignore why we have this problem to begin with: What are the root causes? Why since the appearance of industrialization did alcohol start becoming a problem that has gotten progressively worse? Now it's cocaine.

AA being as it is, a strictly no-controversy, don't-rock-the-boat, no-politics, no-nothing—which I realize was a survival tactic —makes it very convenient for people responsible for coming up with domestic policy and whatnot to ignore problems. It's not only a problem in the U.S.; it seems to be a problem in almost any industrialized country, I think it's consumerism, and a lot of other factors—people leading really unnatural lives—but it's treated like, "We have this Alcoholics Anonymous and we have all these 12 Steps—now we have ACOA, Gamblers Anonymous, you name it—and movie stars and famous people coming out and saying that they'd gotten sober. From reading the newspaper, the problem is obviously not getting better, but we are patting ourselves on the back and saying, "Gee, isn't it wonderful! So-and-so's wife was an alcoholic and she finally came out of the closet and admitted it!''

So, if anything can have a fresh approach or allow a different philosophy, a different way of looking at this, it certainly has my support. I intend to go to the SOS meetings from now on. I'm really hesitant about making a total break with AA because it's so widespread. I found in traveling it's very handy, to make an AA connection—I can talk the talk. Basically, I'm not a hypocrite. For me, the name of the game is staying sober, and I've noticed that people with any kind of long-term sobriety are interested in the same things I am: people who don't drink and don't use drugs.

Sam: Thanks, Kenneth. I've already noted your dry date—we'll have a celebration if you're good.

Mary—did you have something you wanted to share with us?

Mary: Although I don't look it, I'm 75 years old, and I've been sober for nine-and-a-half years. I was born in Pennsylvania, and I had one brother who was five years older then I. We lived in Pennsylvania until I was 13, and then we moved to New York. My father was very, very much against alcohol. Dad was a teetotaler; he belonged to a thing called the Anti-Saloon League. He never said, "You shouldn't ever drink"—he just assumed that you didn't do that sort of thing. When Prohibition was repealed, I was underage, but my brother wasn't, and he very quickly became an alcoholic. As soon as I was old enough, we began to go to bars together. There was a lot of experimenting then, right after Prohibition, quite a heavy bit of drinking. I cooperated with having fun and having a good time and going up during intermission at dances and after dances to have a drink or so, and [I] think it wouldn't have got particularly excessive, [but] a lot of people then were very upset because kids could drink, and they weren't happy about it. My father, of course, found out about it pretty fast. We lived near a business street, and there was a bar there, and he knew that I went over there with [dates] and that sort of thing.

My brother was quite into drinking and was really an alcoholic, but I never had any particular problem, until after I was married and on my own. I figured that nobody had any say in what I could do or not do then, and we had parties occasionally at our house, and we went to parties with other people. My husband and I both thought we could have a drink when we wanted to and could afford it. This went on pretty steadily—not heavily or frequently—until about in the 1960s sometime, we both found that we were with a bunch of people whose main drive was to have a party for whatever reason: somebody got out of the hospital after breaking a leg, and we decided that was a good reason to have a party; or almost anything else that came along. We also—a lot of us together—went to conventions where there was as much drinking as there was making resolutions to improve things. It got pretty heavy for several years in there. Once in a while my husband and I would decide we would probably cut down, and we really did to some extent, or we said, "Only on Monday, Wednesday, and Friday, between nine-thirty and eleven at night," or something like that.

Along in the late seventies, one of my sons . . . wrote me a letter and said he thought when he came to visit us at Christmas time, he and his brothers would like to talk to us about how much we were drinking. At about that time I had gone to the doctor after having had a physical, and he had mentioned to me that my liver wasn't functioning too well. I mentioned to him that I thought I was trying to cut down on drinking, and he said, "Well, that would be a good idea. It may be one reason you're having this trouble with your liver. If you get uptight, take some tranquilizers." He gave me a prescription for some [and added], "and try not to drink." And I would be very careful when I went to parties, but I wasn't particularly careful at home. When I was having trouble sleeping I'd wake up in the middle of the night and I'd decide, "Well, a nice drink is what I need because it will make me sleep better." Even though out in society I appeared not to be having too many drinks, I was doing it at home alone at night and probably consuming just about as much as ever.

In 1982, in January, I became very, very depressed, and I went into the hospital for depression. I was there for three or four weeks, and there wasn't too much talk then about alcohol as a contributing factor. I was sort of confused in my mind anyway, and not really very alert, and I decided that I [hadn't] heard what the doctor said, and that he didn't tell me everything. But he was quite aware that I was having physical difficulties, probably from excessive alcohol consumption. He recommended that I go to a treatment center, which I was very much against at that time. A volunteer, I think, at the hospital when I was there— a very avid AA person—got the big blue book from someplace and gave it to me to read while I was in there. I did, and I told my husband that I read it, and it was full of an awful lot of garbage. For the last thirty or so years I had been considering myself a non-, at least not a, Christian, and probably leaning pretty much toward being a secular person. I never put a name to it, but I decided I was at least not a Christian. So this was why I decided that the AA big book was full of garbage.

I went to a treatment center for thirty days, and in the treatment center, unfortunately, they found out my religious views and kept being very anxious about whether I was getting along with my higher power and that sort of thing. They kept giving me things like, "You can worship a stone or a light bulb," or any of that stuff. They were very, very into AA in the treatment. Even at that time, in fact, they had meetings right there in the treatment center—I think it was twice or three times a week— and you were forced to go to them whether you wanted to or not. All of this bothered me. Also in the AA literature they try very hard to make you feel guilty and wormlike. I was already depressed, and I didn't think that was a very good way to cheer me up, but I decided that I would go along with it. The treatment center had a rule that you should cover the first 5 steps of AA before you got out of the place (I don't know what they did to the people if they didn't). Anyway, I thought, "Well, I won't have a closed mind. I will do what they say. Maybe they're right. At least I will look at it with an open mind, and do the first 5 steps," which probably didn't do me any harm, but I was feeling very badly about their doing me very much good. However, I was quite sure I saw no reason that I would start drinking again. It didn't seem to me that I would. I wasn't concerned about it. All the other people with me when they were being treated kept saying, "What are we going to do when we get out? How are we going to stay away from the stuff?" And I did make up my mind that when I got out, I would skip a couple of the most blatant groups that I belonged to who would have dinners together where they didn't do anything much but drink. I thought I better just stay away from them.

Anyway, I got out, and was never really particularly tempted to take a drink again. I was quite concerned about my physical problem, as well as admitting that my depression would [worsen] because of alcohol. All of the time I was drinking I very seldom blacked out or couldn't remember being some place, even when I did I had [only] a vague memory of them. Early on I used to have morning hangovers, but I didn't in later years—probably didn't give myself a chance to have one. Eventually I stayed sober and never took another drink, but part of the program was to attend AA meetings. So I said, "All right. I'll attend these things. There are millions of them around. You can go any time of the day or night. And I will go."

I went quite regularly, maybe four or so times a week for a while, then I got down eventually to two particular meetings that I thought were pretty good, and once in a while somebody I knew would call me up and we would go to another, so I must have gone to two or three hundred meetings in a couple of years. And they kept saying at the meetings, "This is not religious. You will find the power. Just stick with it." And they kept saying a lot of things that didn't seem to be happening to me. . . . Eventually I said to myself, "What am I doing here? I'm being true to myself, and I'm acting out a lie, and I'm encouraging myself and other people to carry on with something that I think is not what they say it is." I didn't approve of this: of making you feel like a worm, of part of the philosophy as well as the religious connotations. [I] began to wonder what Jewish people and Hindu people and other people like that thought when they went to AA meetings, which were Christian in nature. So I just dropped out after a couple of years and don't go at all anymore.

I didn't go to any kind of meeting until I ran across the article about the Secular Organizations for Sobriety in the *UU World* back in 1988. I began to investigate SOS, thinking, "Ah, I'm glad to know that there is this program around, and hooray for the people who have thought it out!" That's the way I feel, and [I'm] sure there are other people out there who feel the same way. If we got the word around to people they wouldn't have to go through some of the stuff that we had gone through to stay sober. . . .

Having listened to other people who describe their problem, I feel that there are many, many people who are addicted to alcohol. . . . When we have meetings that take the religious issues out of the recovery program in any kind of addiction, it's going to be helpful for a lot of people who are otherwise not going to be helped at all. . . .

Sam: Thanks, Mary. I know your support will be helpful to us all.

Hal? You seem eager to speak.

Hal: I'm Hal, I'm 65 years old, and I've been sober for thirty-five, no, almost thirty-six years. I was born in central Texas, in a farmhhouse, [on] a sandy land farm, the youngest of four children. My parents were farmers, and my father was a pretty hard drinker. . . . He was a maverick—[a] drop-out, and sort of a spoiled brat, and a drinker, as I said. He continued his drinking with periodic episodes of dryness, enforced by threats from my mother to kick him out or leave him several times. He died at the age of 72 with a wet brain. He didn't even know his own children— he didn't recognize us in person nor did he know that we were the ones in [the] pictures by his bed where he lay for the last couple of years of his life. I had a good example of why not to drink right before me, and I vowed that I never would because of all the hell he raised with his family, and all the hardship he caused us.

However, I, like my two older brothers, became hard drinkers, just about like he was. We weren't mean like he was, but we drank just as hard as he ever did. All three of us alcoholics. Both of my older brothers died at an early age, one of them—my oldest brother—at age 37 after a spree to Mexico: he got a lung infection down there and died from that. My next oldest brother committed suicide at the age of 42. He was a hard drinker, too, and while he wasn't drunk at the time he killed himself, his judgment was so impaired that he thought his family had turned against him. He just told them, "Well then, I'll get out of your way," and he went in another room and killed himself—a direct result of impaired judgment due to drinking.

I drank until the age of 29. In 1955 I finally hit bottom good. I couldn't hardly get out of bed in the morning, I was so sick every day. I started attending AA meetings about August of 1955, and it took me until December to finally pick up on what they were talking about and get my brain in operating order. I was drinking all the time I was going to these meetings, but I had spaces in that three or four months there where I sobered up a little bit. Finally, on December 10 of 1955 I either quit drinking or I had my first full day of sobriety—I can't tell you which. I count December 10 as my sobriety date.

It took me a couple of years before I stopped thinking about drinking every single minute of every day that I was awake—and probably dreaming about it when I was asleep. Finally it just faded away like a train whistle in the night—got dimmer and dimmer and dimmer, the yen for a drink. All of a sudden I would realize that it had been maybe two or three weeks or a month since I had even thought about drinking anything. It took me another three or four years to get myself oriented, my mind cleared out enough of the jungle and mess that I had created in it over the years, [so I] could start thinking about how I was going to live. That was the starting place for my beginning to grow up, I guess. At age 29 I was roughly a 16- or 17-year-old kid, because I stopped growing when I started drinking—at least that's the way I view it. There I was, a 30-year-old man with [the] mind and emotions and outlook of a teenage kid, and I've had to build on that. Maybe now, at age 65, I've got the outlook and intellect and emotional makeup of a 50-year-old—but I don't think that's a real hindrance. I'm enjoying life, and I have friends, and I'm generally satisfied with the state of affairs I'm in right now.

I went into AA knowing a whole lot about it. It was kind of scary to me, going and being with *that* kind of people. Even though I knew I was a mess, a drunk in those days was considered to be somebody who didn't have a job, [who] sat around on the curb at street corners and panhandled. They hung out in bars, drinking what other people left sitting on the bar or on tables, that kind of thing: just a general skid-row bum type. It was a small town where I first went to an AA meeting, and I worked in a very classy store there, and some of the finest people in town came in that store. And, lo and behold, here I saw them up here at this AA meeting. It was a big surprise to me that they knew me. I guess half a dozen of them there knew me, and I knew them, casually, and that sort of upset my mental apple cart, because that didn't fit the picture. Remember this is 1955, and we didn't have the same view of AA, or of alcoholics, that's generally held today by the public at large.

So I attended those meetings, and I stayed sober for two or three weeks. In the meantime I had taken another job up-river in the Rio Grande Valley, and I got another job—a better one—up the river a little way. I went up there, and lasted about a week there before I started drinking. . . .

The first thing I did was get in touch with the four AA members who were in the town. . . . They were all Catholics. I was the only non-Catholic there. They said rosaries [and were] very religious. And I began to wonder a little bit, "Was this going to work for me?" I didn't have any such beliefs. They told me to pray for understanding, that I was confused. . . . As time went on I could see that I was. I was learning that my life was unmanageable. I had accepted the first half of that step, the first step, that I was powerless over alcohol, but I hadn't swallowed the fact that my life was absolutely unmanageable.

So I stayed with it, and as time went on I did perceive that my life had been unmanageable and still was. If I hadn't had a pretty solid wife who knew how to run things, my whole family would have fallen apart, I guess. But hanging on to the AA meetings and listening to these people discuss how God guided them through every day and kept them from yielding to their temptations to go back to drinking—I knew that there wasn't any outside force keeping them from doing anything; that whatever they did, they did it from within themselves; and whatever it was that they had, I, being another human being like them, could do it, too. All I had to do was figure out what it was they were doing and do it myself. That was when I stopped drinking. I learned that the thing they did was to do the 12 Steps; and I started in on that. That was the day that I stopped drinking: when I decided that I would do something—anything—to solve this problem.

When I would come to the parts about turning my life over to a God as I understood him, and to higher powers, I just sort of skirted that, and then I came across the one that used the term, "a power greater than myself." I knew there were powers greater than I was. Everyone of those other members in AA had power greater than I had because they didn't drink, and I was having a terrific problem trying to keep from drinking. So anybody else there that had one day more than I had [of] sobriety was a power greater than I was, or possessed power greater than I possessed. That's sort of the way I decided to look at it: that the group or particular individuals within the group would be my power greater than myself, the one I would rely on to help me get sober and stay sober. And it worked. I knew there wouldn't [be] an intervening supernatural power, and from the beginning I didn't try to pretend that there was one. However, they told me to pray for understanding. Well I sort of repeated to myself, made up little things as I'd be driving to work or coming home from work or while I was working at my workbench, I would recite over in my mind things that I heard them say. I guess you would call it nowadays, psychobabble, positive reinforcement, or such things as that, by repetition of these things that, to me, amounted to what they called "prayer to a divine intercessor." To me it was just a psychological exercise. And it worked. I guess that's what worked, because I haven't drunk anything since.

I attended AA meetings regularly for about five or six years, and then my children were getting up [to] school age, and I sort of dropped out [of] AA, and didn't attend for about fourteen years. . . . Then I read the article in *Free Inquiry* about SOS. I contacted SOS by phone, talked about it, and another fellow locally here . . . got together and started [to] meet on an SOS basis. We have very small meetings, but [they're] here for anybody who wants it.

SOS and AA are interchangeable to me, because I'm not offended by all of the references to God, to *a* God, I'll put it that way. We've sort of agreed here that we always used the article in front of the word *G-o-d*. We tell people that they're welcome at our meetings if they're believers, but they leave their God outside before they walk in the door. Leave any God that they have outside. We always use a qualifier in front of *God* to show that it's their God, it's not a generic God, a *real* one that presides over everything. And if they want to talk about such matters, they go somewhere else. . . .

I've noticed that most new people who come in have an emotional build-up from having attended AA meetings against religious talk in meetings, and they'll spend their first meeting or two berating what goes on at AA meetings. They say they get sick of it, and they're offended by it, and [that] they get so frustrated having to listen to it that some of them say they've gotten up and stomped out of AA meetings. . . . After a couple of meetings, they get that over with, and then they'll settle down to talking about real life issues and start to try to figure out how to build a new way of living based on the principles that SOS presented to them. . . .

There are about three different kinds of people that we get. One type is pretty clear-minded about just wanting some place to go to solve his or her problem with alcohol or drugs, without the irrelevances of higher powers intervening and all of that, because they just don't believe such things exist. They're very serious about wanting to get down to the nitty-gritty of the problem that's inside themselves and solve it from within with help from us.

Another kind is a militant atheist who wants to come to the meetings and get started right away on doing something about the religion in the schools: it's being shoved down their children's throats at schools. I tell them that's not what this is all about. They've got a drinking problem, all right, but they've got this organization mixed up with some other organization that they wish they could find, which is a political, militant attack on religion being imposed on their children in schools, or maybe on themselves at work. We have to tell them, "Well, that's not what this is all about. This is about solving your problem with whatever addictive drug you're taking."

Another one is not really a nonbeliever or even an agnostic. They're believers who are mad at whatever God they actually believe exists, or whatever church they belong to. They've had something bad happen to them, and they come and want to cuss that out real good and get that off of their chest, and then they're sort of through with us. They're like the person whose child gets run over and killed out in front of their house, and they've been churchgoing believers all their lives—thoroughly Baptist, thoroughly Catholic, or whatever—and they say, "Oh there can't be a God. No real God would let anything like this happen to me." That's clearly [a] self-centered view of things. It didn't happen to the kid, it happened to them.

That's what I've noticed about new members. . . .

Sam: Thanks, Hal. I think you've given us something to think and talk about while we break for coffee, tea, and some cookies (baked them myself). We'll resume the meeting in about fifteen or twenty minutes. (By the way, restrooms are down the hall to the left.)

*   *   *

Sam: Are we all seated comfortably again?

Kyla, are you ready to contribute?

Kyla: I'm Kyla, I'm 34 years old, and I've been sober for five years. Born in Arizona. I'm the oldest of four. I came from a family that didn't abuse anything, really, except food. Abusing alcohol was just not acceptable. When I was a kid, I watched my mom trying to stay thin on diet pills and coffee and cigarettes and all those good kinds of things. I decided very early on that I'd never do that to myself.

Got married to get out of the house at 21, which was a real bad mistake. My weight until then had not been—I'd been chunky but not really fat. In the two years [of] my first marriage I put on sixty pounds. Trying to get through school—working during the day and going to school at night—I put on about another forty. Ended up, just a few weeks before I graduated, closer to three hundred pounds than I ever want to admit. And it was at this point, do something or die! Up until then I'd only done two diets in my life. One of them was Weight Watchers, which I promptly flunked out of at the age of 13; and the other was a doctor-supervised fast, which didn't work.

A year after that I got into 12-steps recovery programs, and after three years there, something started nagging, just nagging at the back of my head, saying, "Wait a minute!" I was a prototypical good girl—some people call [us] doormats. I didn't lie, cheat, steal, to afford my habit. And I'm going, "Wait a minute!" What do I have to make amends to people for? [I] got into some other therapy work in conjunction with that, where I found out that throughout my lifetime I was a survivor of just about everything that's been done or can be done in this society to mess up a young girl's mind, and I'd been using food to push it down.

About six months ago I read an article in the SOS *Newsletter* that talked about the problems with 12-step programs for survivors of childhood abuse. And it's like, "That's me! Where's the nearest meeting?" I've been going there ever since. It's much more, for me, in keeping with my needs, because I've learned that I'm the one responsible for keeping me sober, sane, abstinent —whatever you want to call it—that you don't use no matter what. For a lot of my recovery in the 12-step programs, that hadn't really been an emphasis. It's something I'm very grateful to SOS for, because in a way I was alone in that, like, I don't cross these lines no matter what. The people in SOS understood that. The people in OA didn't. Like, "Well, you want it? Go out and eat it and start all over again." Like, you don't understand, I don't mess with this stuff.

I've gone through a lot in my recovery. I'm down about a hundred pounds. I've been hoarding the same clothes for four years, which I've learned enough to do, because [as] a compulsive eater I was used to wearing a new size every season, either up or down. If things were going well, then I'd have to go replace everything in the closet with a smaller size. If things weren't going so well, it's roll it all out and get some bigger clothes. Well, I've been wearing the same clothes for four years now. That's something I don't think any female in my family has ever done, because they're all constantly on diets. I don't have to do that.

I've done a lot of things that amount to risk taking that I couldn't have done without starting a recovery program of one sort or another. And I've learned some lessons along the way. One of them is that the world out there is not a nice place, and just because the world is not a nice place doesn't mean you mess with your recovery. That's the one thing I will always have. That's dependent on me. . . . I go now to family things and I watch my family, all of whom are in denial about whatever their respective problems are. I just get to be grateful that I'm not joining the family tradition of a hundred or a hundred-and-fifty pound a year weight swings, up and down. I come to family parties and say, "Oh, gee. You're on a fast? So you're not eating this week." Or the ones who've just come off diets bingeing on anything in sight—knowing I don't have to do that's a pretty neat feeling.

I've made some good friends. I've learned a lot of things in SOS, because this isn't a game. This is life and death. If I screw up I'm going to die. And not all of it is the just-think-of-it-and-go-back-to-three-hundred pounds. That wouldn't be an immediate death sentence. What would be is that some of the restrictions I'm on are medical: there are certain foods my body doesn't like. In SOS when I say, "I just can't mess with these things," they understand. I don't mess with grains the way they don't mess with booze. It doesn't mean you don't feel deprived, and it doesn't mean you don't feel different sometimes. You still don't get to use. That to me has been the beauty of recovery, that I don't have to use. I can walk through this stone-cold sober. I don't have to be drunk on Twinkies or anything else.

I'm an engineer by training and telling me that the supernatural is going to do this for me, for me just didn't make it. In SOS I can say that "Yeah, it's your choice. Take it or leave it." And I decided to take it. The only thing that I regret is that there aren't more meetings in this area, because I would dearly love to be able to go to three or four meetings a week, and there just aren't that many that fit in my schedule. We talked about it one night at a meeting, and we came to the conclusion that the stronger the bible belt is in that area, the more SOS meetings there are. Since this isn't a bible-thumping area, we don't have as many—don't *need* as many—meetings, I guess is the way someone put it.

But it's been neat. I've been able to do the things I've had to do in the last five years to grow up. I've joined my professional society, making a name for myself at work. I'm looking for a new job, when I realized this one wasn't the place I was supposed to be.

Being sober has given me back a life. In some ways it's a life I never had growing up. It's not easy, but I'm doing things today that have to be done, and I can look back on it, and [say], "Yeah, I did that, and I can be proud of it." I can also tackle things I don't like to do, like doing paperwork—which is funny because I deal with paper for a living. But my own paperwork at home piles up. So I can take a day like I did today, and just sit down and, "OK, I'm not going to stop until the table is clear." And I'm almost there. It's not supernatural or anyone else doing it for me; it's me sitting down at that damned table and clearing it. I've just about done it.

Recovery has meant I'm a different person. I've associated along the way with people who aren't in recovery programs in the last five years, and I've gotten to see how much I've changed in relationship to them. I don't whine anymore. I'm not a doormat anymore. My family doesn't know what to do with me, because I've learned to "Just say no," as the saying goes. "This is not acceptable behavior and I will not tolerate it anymore." They don't understand. And it's OK. I'm not out to make converts. But it feels good to know that I can be an adult and not a whining harpie. That's something else I've done in recovery. I've become an adult. An adult is someone who just does the things that have to be done without whining about it. I've learned some other things. Came up with one at a meeting a few weeks ago, that I don't binge anymore because it's just too goddamn much trouble. I wasn't thinking about it till after I said [it], and every[one] else picked up on the line. It's true. It's just too much trouble to even think about going out there again. . . . And that was really neat to know that I've come to the conclusion there's just too much trouble to go out again. So I don't do it. And to know that in the five years it's taken me to get there, it's become ingrained in my brain that I just don't do this anymore. That loser brain has been retrained. It's not an option. It can be done. It takes time, and it takes persistence, and it takes a willingness to admit that you don't have all the answers, and the only answer you have for today is to stay sober. And when the loser brain gets told "No" enough times, it eventually shuts up.

There are times that it tries to come back, when I'm under extreme stress or something like that. But like I told you once, I told you twice, "No, go away." It ain't worth the bother. And that's what it's become. Recovery is life, and bingeing, or the using, just isn't worth the bother. . . .

Sam: Thank you, Kyla. Although there are all varieties of addiction, maintaining the Sobriety Priority can lead to recovery in all cases. Thanks, again.

Now, George—What's on your mind?

George: I'm George, 64 years old, and sober since November 17, 1983. I was born on Christmas Eve in 1926. I'm one of five children, and I have one sister and three brothers, initially, that grew to adulthood. My older brother was an alcoholic for many years and drifted in and out. He went to AA several times. None of the other people in my family—including my parents, to the best of my knowledge—were alcoholics. They just drank moderately.

My first recollection of having anything to drink at all was when I was about 12 or 13. There was a summer picnic ground and a bunch of us young boys found out that on Sundays, occasionally when they had picnics, toward the end of the day the doors were left open and there were lots of pitchers of beer still laying around on the tables. That was my first introduction to alcohol and I thought it was great.

I went away in the Navy when I was 17 and proceeded to consume alcohol because that seemed to be the thing to do. Whenever you got out on leave on a pass on a weekend, you'd go down to the local place and illegally get somebody to get you something to drink.

Then I got married. Interestingly enough, I cut down my alcoholic consumption to almost nothing. We had five kids, and we were so hand-to-mouth trying to make ends meet that nothing ever happened.

In the sixties I got heavily involved in politics in a New York metropolitan area. The little meetings were held in bars and I just got into it more heavily and more heavily. Finally it got to the point where one of the things I thought of a great deal was "Where am I going to get my next drink?" I can remember being involved in going to parties and fundraising things, and by then I'd graduated to the point where I couldn't just come home from work and go to the dinner and whatever and have a few drinks at the open bar. I had to have two or three drinks quickly before I left, to fortify me, to make sure that I was in good shape to go someplace to start drinking. I guess at that point I faintly thought maybe I might have a problem.

I transferred to the West Coast with my company in 1979. In February of that year I had a company physical, including a complete blood work-up. A couple of weeks [later] the doctor called me back in and he said, "It's quite obvious from the results of your blood test that you have a very serious alcohol problem. All the indications are that you're on the verge of completely ruining your body. And you have three choices. Either you can go to a rehab over in Arizona someplace; or you can go to an AA meeting today; or you're fired." That really got my attention because I'd been with the company over thirty years. My little pea brain immediately said, "Go to AA, because that's the least of the problems, and you'll get the company off your back. You don't want to lose your job, because then you won't have any money to buy the booze anymore." I never really, at that point, thought that I was ever going to get sober, but they really got my attention.

I went to AA because that's all there was in 1979. That

was the only place you could go. I went to meetings almost daily for six months. Took another company physical—mandatory—and all of the readings on my terrible, terrible blood readings were almost miraculously back to within normal limits. That said to me, "I no longer have a problem," and then very shortly [after] I stopped going to meetings. Three months later I had my first drink—a can of beer—and within a couple of months I was back to drinking as much as I had in the past.

In November of 1983 I finally called the local AA number, and they said, "There's a meeting in two days in your area." And I went. How I stayed sober for those two days I don't know. I guess I had finally had enough. I was sick and tired of being sick and tired, I guess. I was drinking over a quart of Scotch, plus about a fifth of white wine every day. And that's all I did, all day long, sit around and drink—and not really enjoying it very much anymore. But my body physically—I had a habit. I couldn't live without my liquor.

I went to AA and blamed everybody else for my problems —the pressure of my job, my family—it was everybody else's fault but mine. I was sober, but I was still in tremendous denial. Where I come from a lot of the AA meetings are very, very fundamentalist in that many, many people at the meetings tell you how to be: you have to get down on your knees and pray every night and thank God that you're sober and thank Him in the morning when you get up that here's another day and I'm going to stay sober through your help. And that has never been my forte—believing in those things—and I got increasingly upset about it. The Lord's Prayer at the end of every meeting, when we all held hands, really got me annoyed. Finally in 1988 I read an article in the Unitarian magazine about SOS and Jim Christopher, and I had the good luck of calling him on the phone and finding out about his book. And I read the book and said to myself, "Hallelujah! Where have you been all my life?" I agree with everything that's said in the book, and it's the most wonderful thing that has happened to me, is finding out about SOS.

That winter I went to Florida, and the first SOS meetings I went to were down there with a wonderful bunch of people. Then we came back to Western New York, and I refused to go to an AA meeting again. And I talked to Jim Christopher, and he said, "Well, you know, if there are no meetings down where you live, there's an alternative: Start your own meeting." So a couple of years ago we started an SOS meeting in July of '89, and the meeting's been going ever since. Now there are three SOS meetings in my area. I think the most wonderful thing that's happened to me is being able to get into this group of friendly and nonjudgmental people whose priority is staying sober, not holding hands and doing all those other things that the other group seems to insist on doing in order to stay sober—which is, of course, patently not true. . . .

Sam: Thank you, George. I hope we can count on you to promote this Tuesday SOS meeting—you seem to have some good ideas. You can count on us to remember and celebrate your dry date. Anyone else?

Susan?

Susan: I'm Susan, 56 years old, sober for three years. Well, I was born in Nebraska in a German Lutheran ghetto, I like to call it, on the farm, so all I was exposed to growing up was the Lutheran Church. My family wasn't rabidly religious but they were cold, unaffectionate people. They would tell me that they loved me like crazy, but I don't think they ever really liked me. I was the youngest of two. My sister was seven years older, and we lived far enough from town that when it came time for us to go to high school, we were boarded out with strangers—rooms were rented out for us to go and stay in. So we not only were torn away from home at 13, but we also really didn't have a support system during that very crucial time in our life. My sister was basically gone from the time I was 5, so I had the burdens of the youngest and oldest child, the personality things, you know. I think my parents never got along real well—there was always tension in the house. Even my sister admits that they say one child is the repository of the craziness in a marriage, and I was it, because she was basically gone before things got really bad.

I was a binge drinker, and I think I drank solely to have fun, guilt-free. A lot of people drink for other reasons, but as I look back, that's my basic one. I was never supposed to have a good time. My parents would even frequently tell me, "You like to have too good a time." "You don't take things seriously enough." Even as a child, if I set out to do something, I got a list of admonitions to look out for so that I didn't get hurt, didn't get my clothes dirty, didn't embarrass my parents—. We got told what we could say before we left home. I could never have fun. It was always this horrible guilt trip, and fear trip, so I think that as soon as the first time that I drank—I was a senior in high school—I got drunk, I had a blackout, and I told off a couple of my friends that I had big resentments about. There was your first clue: That was my first time drunk.

Our family always required us to be the honor students and to be first in our class, so of course I was. I graduated first in my class of a hundred and thirty-four, I think. This, while boarding out in town, having my own bank account, and handling my own personal life, on my own, from Monday through Friday. Then my folks elected to send me to a Lutheran college, where we had to be in our own rooms at seven-thirty every night, and I thought this was, quite patently, bullshit. I had been on my own for four years and now to be told that I had to be locked up, I couldn't smoke, I couldn't drink, I couldn't even go to another person's room after seven-thirty at night. I frankly thought it was a crock, and I think that that instituted a rebellion I would not otherwise have had.

Drinking was absolutely forbidden—even if you were caught drinking off campus, at the school it meant imminent expulsion. I, of course, climbed out the windows and went drinking, had a good time. And very nearly got expelled, but I didn't. But I quit after two-and-a-half years because I just couldn't see struggling along in this college. I wanted to be an engineer, . . . but there were three career options in those days: nurse, secretary, teacher. I didn't like kids, so that left me with secretary.

My drinking was always party drinking. After three drinks I was totally out of control, and then I'd wake up and be not only horribly, horribly sick, but also would have horrible guilt, because drinking's frowned upon in my family. It allowed me to have this wonderful guilt-free time when I was drunk, then the next morning, of course, the guilt presented its face. This was pretty much the pattern of my drinking in college.

I was 23 when I got married the first time into a hard-drinking family—a violent family. One of them even tried to blame the problems in our marriage on my drinking, totally ignoring their own drinking. It's interesting that a family's alcoholics even then thought that perhaps I was drinking too much. That was a very short marriage, because he was violent.

Then I married a much older man who was also an alcoholic. I didn't know what an alcoholic was. I had this weird moral code that said if a woman was married she shouldn't smoke or drink, so after that first marriage, I really embraced this code. . . . When I married the second one, he drank a lot and it scared me, so I pulled back and was the responsible one who made sure everything got done. Ten years into that marriage, I was a basket case and so I went to Al-Anon. This was my exposure to 12-step programs. I had read about it in the paper, and actually quit my job so that I could go to Al-Anon in the daytime so that my husband wouldn't find out. I knew how angry he would be.

In Al-Anon, on one hand, they saved my life; on the other they did more damage to me. They told me I had to believe in a higher power, and that part was difficult for me. But I was so desperate and so low and so down by this time I would have done anything they said to feel better, because my heart was so broken by this alcoholic whom I was so crazy about and who was puking all over me. Finally they said, "Use anything." So I decided, "OK, I'll use this mountain as my Higher Power."

Then they started to subtly pooh-pooh that. They tell you to use an inanimate object, and when you do they subtly start to tell you that you should put that over to God. Finally I got into Unity, the most palatable of the religions that I could find. Unity gave me a lot of good stuff to live by, [but] I finally left Unity because the God of the deepest subject got to be too much for me. . . . Unity Church did me no harm and did me a lot of good. . . . For a while they made my life bearable.

After several leavings and coming back, my husband quit drinking on his own for about three months. Then he started drinking again and went on this binge where he was gone for four days. When he came back, he said, "I'll quit. . . . I went to one of *your* AA meetings. And all they talked about was God. And you know I don't believe in God." . . . How could I ask him to go to a recovery program that ran contrary to everything that he basically believed in?

Right about that time we separated, [but] we kept seeing each other. Six months later he drove his pick-up truck on the road about a quarter mile from my house and blew his brains out. And at the time it occurred to me that there ought to be something for somebody who didn't believe in God.

I got married again to a guy who had twenty years of sobriety in AA. So I went with him to AA meetings but never went as an AA person myself. I didn't, at that time, think I was an alcoholic, because, once I married him, he didn't drink, I didn't drink. I quit for six-and-a-half years on my own. But I listened to all this stuff, and I remember . . . I thought that it was screwed up! I remember sitting there and thinking, "If I ever need this for myself, down the road, there'll have to be something else." First of all, I think the AA "Big Book" is just really a dumb and horribly written book; it's literally sophomoric. I felt, as a woman, that the 12 steps were demeaning. We do not need more humility, more apologizing, more subservience. Women alcoholics have already been totally subservient and constantly apologizing and humble right down to the floor. And so I didn't like that part of it.

Anyway, after six-and-a-half years of sobriety, life was not any fun. We didn't have a social life. My husband was basically antisocial. When we did go out, we went out with other AA people. All they talked about, when they got together socially, was who was cheating on his wife and therefore going to slip; who had a bad attitude and was therefore going to slip; who had slipped; who wasn't working their program; who was working their program. It was boring. One day I decided life was no fun, and I decided to have some guilt-free fun again and started to drink. And I was at a wedding and somebody said, "Champagne?" And I said, "You bet!" I was angry, so I started to drink.

I divorced the husband, and then I got into a really bad three-year relationship with a married guy—who, of course, was an alcoholic. He and I had three years of a lot of fun drinking and an awful lot of pain because he was married, and during that time I read in *Free Inquiry* about SOS. I said to myself, "One of these days I am going to quit again, and when I do, I'm going to start one of these SOS groups."

I had a friend at that time, Vic, who was wheelchair-bound, and he was drinking too much, too. Occasionally we'd get drunk together and we'd say, "We've got to quit. We've got to quit." Finally, after three years of this affair, I was out visiting this guy in New York, and we started to push each other around—not hit each other, but push each other around—and this was totally foreign to my values. The next morning I said, "This has gone too far. I am going to go home, and I'm going to quit drinking, and I'm going to try to forget about you. This is a bad situation. I shouldn't get involved with somebody married anyway. And so this is it."

I went home and called up Vic and told him what I had done. I said, "I'm leaving for the summer, now, and so when I get back in the fall, you and I are going to start this group." When I got back in September, [I] called [Vic] up, put some ads in the paper, and called SOS for some names, and got them. Vic and I started to sit in a local restaurant, and we sat there alone for three or four weeks. . . . Now we have three meetings in our area and I'm thinking about a fourth. . . .

I like SOS because they tell us it's OK to have a good self-image. We aren't supposed to be constantly beating our breast and derogating ourselves. It's OK to feel good about ourselves. SOS believes that a good self-image is crucial to recovery, it's OK to have fun in our lives. Now I can have guilt-free fun sober. The people who come believe that, and so, of course, we're with like-minded people for the most part. After three years I still go because it's a reminder. I remember that not going to meetings for six-and-a-half years I forgot how bad it was. When I got bored and unhappy and life wasn't any fun, the only way I knew to go and have fun was to get drunk—and I forgot how bad it was. So I kept going to meetings so that I didn't ever forget how bad it was. And it's fun; it just makes it all worthwhile. . . .

Another thing I like about SOS is they don't tell us how to run every facet of our life. SOS assumes that we have the intelligence within ourselves to know how we ought to run our life once we get sober, so that we have the capacity to make decisions for ourselves. They give us some credit for having some intelligence.

. . . Here's something that I said that is a phrase: "I believe that an abiding fixation on humility is detrimental to happy sobriety." I do believe that. As rational thinking people we should be able to pat ourselves on the back for realizing somewhere in our drinking career that normal people don't live like this, and then doing something about it. We should give ourselves credit for being here right now instead of in the bar or at home with a bottle of whatever we drink. I think it's healthful, not harmful, to tell ourselves each day that we are worthwhile persons, no matter what our past drinking life may have entailed.

It's a whole lot healthier to say I'm a pretty neat person, than to keep saying how awful we are. That's one of the things I really like about SOS—we're not expected to beat our breasts and play "Can-you-top-this" about how rotten we are. . . .

Sam: That's an excellent point, Susan: that we should give ourselves credit for what we are—what we've become—rather than bemoan what we were. Thank you.

Do you have something to say, Martin?

Martin: I'm Martin. I've been sober for ten years. I'm 37 years old. I was born in 1954 in Maryland. The fifth of six children, Irish Catholic, went to Catholic school, all that stuff. Learned about God early on. Drinking was always a problem; it was always a part of the environment. Irish Catholic alcoholic. A dysfunctional family. Lots of arguing and fighting, and sometimes there were fists thrown. But growing up I thought it was normal. I didn't know it was abnormal, unhealthy. So I started drinking early on, right from the beginning. And I had problems. I started to do things when I drank that I normally wouldn't do, which meant that I started to embarrass myself and people around me. It was a problem before I drank it, it was a problem right when I started to drink it, and it was a problem my whole life.

I started drinking when I was young—10 or 11 years old—and I started sniffing glue and hanging out with groups of kids who were into the same thing. It always seemed like within the group, I was the worst one, maybe me and somebody else who was exhibiting the worst behavior. We would always hook up and become good drinking buddies.

By the time I was 16 I was drinking every day, taking drugs every day. So I did the normal thing: I quit school; I didn't work. I lived in my parents' home. When they would throw me out, I would always come back. I would get a job, hold it for a couple of months, quit before I got fired. My thing was my work and staying up all night drinking, doing drugs, sleeping all day, and living off my parents. I did it until I was 20 years old. . . . Everybody that I was hanging out with, a lot of them were starting to get lives: they were getting married, they were going into careers, they were progressing. The way normal people were supposed to go. But I didn't. I was still hanging out. I discovered there was nobody else there—I was the only one. So I decided to go into the service, and I went into the Navy. I got on a ship, and as long as we were out at sea I did real well, because I couldn't drink. It was hard to get booze in the middle of the ocean for guys like me. But I got into trouble overseas.

All I did when I was overseas was drink. I went to all these exotic ports and all I saw was the first bar. All these guys I was with were buying cameras, stereos—a lot of them were saving money. I owed everybody money—I was bumming money so I could drink every night in these bars in the Philippines.

When I got back to the United States, I discovered I was going to become a legal yeoman—like a paralegal, I guess—and I got orders to go to school in Mississippi and thirty days' leave and thirty days' advance pay. Instead of going to the school, I discovered Wild Irish Rose. It only cost a buck forty-five a fifth. I decided I wasn't going to go back to the service, so I went on this six-month drunk. Eventually I turned myself in, was court-martialed, and went to jail for a little while. And I remember when I was in jail, I thought, "I'm going to change my life: I'm going to do it different." . . .

When they let me out, I thought, "Now I'm going to change my life," and so I started to hitchhike home. By the time I got there I was drunk already, with seventeen dollars in my pocket. And I did the same thing I had done before. I went home. I lived with my parents. I slept all day. Drank all night. Did drugs all night. Found a new group of people to hang out with, people who were just like me, not doing anything. And I would get a job, hold it for a little while, quit it before I got fired.

The drinking was getting worse. I was getting more and more antisocial. Blackouts were becoming really frequent, an every-night occurrence. And I would say a little prayer, "I know I'm going to black out; I just hope I don't do anything embarrassing." Because I knew I wouldn't remember: there were those horrible feelings of having to walk back into the bar the next night and not know what happened the night before, and of just waiting for this look from the barmaid or the bartender to see how much of an asshole you were.

Eventually I met this girl and we lived together for a while and had a kid. After two o'clock when the bar closed, I would bring the bar home. We would cook breakfast in my apartment and my girlfriend—now my wife—she didn't want to put up with it. We got into a big argument, and I got physical and abused her, so she took the baby and all her possessions—everything—and left. A couple of weeks later I called her and told her I would quit drinking, and I did. I just did drugs. . . .

It was really weird. All these people thought I was doing well. They thought, "He's doing good. All he's doing is eating Quaaludes and smoking dope and eating speed." They thought that was doing good in comparison to drinking. For eight months, I stopped drinking. . . . Then John Lennon and the pope got shot. I was really miserable, and every day I thought about drinking—it was just horrible.

I can remember going to a doctor because I thought I was having a cardiac arrest, and all he said was [it] was nerves. He asked me if anything was on my mind. I told him I had quit drinking, and he didn't advise me to go to recovery or anything like that, but he said, "Yeah, that's a rough thing to go through." At that time I was seeing a counselor for alcoholism where I worked. I had that incident with my wife. I was also on the verge of losing my job. I was into getting paid on a Friday and not coming back till the Wednesday of the next week. I would just go on a drunk and spend my check and not call in or anything. They were holding me accountable for stuff like that.

After eight months of being dry and just doing drugs, nothing was getting better. Because I wasn't drinking, my wife came back and eventually made a call to a couple of guys from AA. . . . The next day they came over and they 12-stepped me in AA and took me to an AA meeting. . . .

We went to this AA meeting, and it kind of clicked. I knew I was at the end of the line. I knew that the drugs were just like the alcohol, that my life wasn't going to change—it was just getting worse. I knew I had to do something. At AA early on, I knew exactly what they were talking about. I knew that the thing was about God and it didn't turn me off—at first. I really tried. I went to meetings every day and I prayed. I read stuff that's considered spiritual literature. I read all their literature. I got into these big discussions with other people. I went on this great spiritual quest. I was going to be an AA guru, but deep down inside it just wasn't happening. I was very frustrated. I was staying sober, and I knew I was staying sober—that was a physical fact—but I was afraid if I didn't get this God thing that I was going to get drunk. So I prayed down on my knees every day for three years, in the morning, and at night. After three years of trying to do it that way, I felt completely false, completely miserable. I was almost, in a way, more miserable than when I was drinking, because then I had experienced a lot of loneliness, but it was because I alienated myself with my actions, with my behavior. This time, I was lonely all over again because I was trying to be a part of something that just wasn't right with me— it wasn't honest.

After three years of trying to do the 12-step way, I just stopped doing it: one night I didn't pray, I just got into my bed. I didn't have any booze in my house, even though I was almost convinced that I was going to wake up drunk the next morning. I don't know why. I guess it was from thousands of meetings and hearing, "If you don't get God in your life, you're going to get drunk." But I didn't wake up drunk; and I didn't get drunk, and I haven't been drunk.

Then the struggle began. It seems I've been struggling my whole life: first, with alcohol and drugs; now with sobriety. For six more years, almost until my ninth year of sobriety, I stood in the AA rooms, I said how I felt. It was such a lonely experience, because I was the only one saying the things that I was saying. And I was sure that other people felt that way, but I wasn't hear-ing them. Nobody else was getting up and saying, "Hey, I don't believe in this God thing. I feel false when I pray." There was absolutely no support there. . . . People would come out and say, "Man, we really appreciate your honesty," but I wanted somebody to come up to me and say, "Hey, man, I feel exactly like you do." People would come up to me and say, "I'll pray for you"—that really went through me. But after a while I started to shut down. . . . I started to feel like a martyr, and I didn't like it. I started to feel alone.

I started to go to fewer meetings. The meetings I went to I would sit behind poles, or if I was called on I would pass. When people asked me to chair meetings, I would say, "No" because I knew that I was going to rock the boat, and I didn't want to. I felt a great debt to AA—people there helped me save my life. They took their time, their energy—there were people there for me. And they're still there in my life today. But I just felt like I was all alone.

An agnostic/atheist meeting that I started to go to was called the Agnostic Group, but it really wasn't much different from the other group. It was almost like they were using the group as the higher power. . . . And this idea was emerging within me that I'm doing this on my own. Essentially, it's up to me.

I would tell the people in AA that the only thing that stands between me and drink is me, and nobody wanted to hear that. *I* didn't want to hear it because it scared me. I had never been responsible in my life. All of a sudden, I am starting to become aware of this truth, and it's scaring me, because what it's saying to me is that I'm responsible for my life—and my actions and my sobriety. But AA was the only game in town, and there was nobody there to share the idea with.

Eventually, I got the book *Unhooked,* and I read it, and thought, "Yeah, this is exactly how I feel."

Finally, I started an SOS group. . . . There were times when I was the only person at the SOS meeting, and that was real frustrating. . . . I wanted this thing to work, and it was frustrating, but eventually it did. Now six people come all the time.

When people first get there, it seems they have to recover from AA, to talk about their experience there. We're real careful with that because we're not into AA-bashing; we're about recovering, or staying recovered—whatever stage you're at.

We took the 12 Steps of AA, and we broke them down, and now we have our own steps that we use, our own guidelines—seven of them—that we use for ourselves.

Since I started the SOS meetings, I've been to a few AA meetings, but it's a social thing, to see friends, people that I know. There's nothing there for me anymore. . . . I consider myself a member of SOS.

For almost nine years I carried this weight on my shoulders of being confused, being alone. As soon as the SOS meeting started, and as soon as it started to kick in, it all went away. Secular sobriety to me now isn't like an afterthought or like a second thought or natural, because there's still a lot we're finding out about it and about ourselves, but it is becoming like a way of life. These few times that I've gone to AA meetings and I've listened to people talk about how to pray, it's almost like I don't even understand it anymore. I don't understand why people would even want to do that. It's so far removed from the way I do things and the way I want to do things. I really have changed in sobriety: I haven't just changed from being a person who drank and did a lot of drugs, but I've *changed* in sobriety. And a lot of that had to do with SOS being available to me.

Six of us show every week, and different people take care of the meeting every week. For a while it was just me, coming in, setting up, paying the bills. Now everybody's starting to kick in, we're like a group. We have kind of a group identity, but we haven't lost our individual identities. . . . I'm with people who on certain things think like me, on a lot of other things, they don't, but when it comes to sobriety and how to achieve it and how to maintain it, we pretty much agree.

Sam: Thank you for sharing your feelings about SOS with us, Martin, and welcome to our group.

Emma?

Emma: I'm 49 years old, and have been sober for seven-and-one-half years. My parents wanted a son to complement my older sister, but instead they got a daughter who would grow up to drink like a man. [I] succeeded in drinking a quart of vodka a day during the last two years of my drinking career, yet was still able to function. Way above average was I. Small towns in the Midwest have dirty farmers, lots of taverns, tall corn, and women alcoholics still in the closet. I escaped Iowa, but not the propensity to look to alcohol for solutions to my problem. A grandfather, four uncles, and my mother sought similar refuge, with devastating results. Some of my earliest memories are of an angry, drinking uncle coming over to the house to castigate my mother. The next morning he would apologize. But I'll never forget my mother saying, "There comes a time when saying 'I'm sorry' doesn't mean anything anymore." I admonished another uncle as he poured more whiskey, "Don't you know that each ounce of that poison is killing thousands of brain cells, never to be replaced?" I was about 8 at the time.

My childhood was filled with constant bitter quarreling in the family. My mother's alcoholism never really blossomed until after I had left home, but both my parents were overworked and very overtired. One morning when my sister and I were still in grade school, our mother told us not to look for her in the kitchen where she usually was when we got home, because she would be upstairs in the attic hanging from the rafters. That's devastating stuff for kids to take. We got the message that children were too time-consuming and brought parents only pain.

I was 17 when I first got drunk with a friend, and I [had] learned to drink plenty of Scotch by the time I got my college diploma. There followed twenty-three years of heavy drinking, until I quit at the age of 42. A [one-time] daily drinker, I now joke that my definition of a *periodic* is someone who doesn't drink in the morning. With seven-and-a-half years of continuous sobriety now, I look back at why I drank.

For many years it was fun. It felt good. I can admit this at SOS meetings without being warned not to make imbibing sound too good, too fun. I loved fancy cocktail lounges. Sexual inhibitions, from years of Catholic priests and nuns telling us sex was filthy, melted away. I think this [is] a problem with many women. I drank simply to feel normal. Along with a great set of legs, I also inherited my mother's perpetual anxiety and nervousness, so I would drink to allay this feeling. Gradually, the very same drinking caused me anxiety attacks, and to be scared. At the end I was afraid of the telephone ringing—I wanted to retreat to my safe little place in the bedroom.

Then I found I couldn't stop drinking. One morning driving home after an early exercise class—prior to which I [had] already had two vodka and orange juices—I thought: "Another day that I have to drink!" I no longer had any choice in the matter. . . . But a complete physical brought to light the warning signs of the start of some serious health problems. On my own, as a result of that scare by the doctor, I quit for eight months and was losing the ugly, bloated look and feeling much better, when, for an anniversary gift, the resort at which my husband and I were staying, left a complimentary bottle of champagne in the room. All the pleasant floating feelings returned with that first chilled glass. It would take quite a few more months of heavy drinking before my husband finally threw a lamp through a picture window in complete frustration. Prior to that time he never said much about my drinking—just "Have a better day!" when he left the house in the morning. We didn't talk. I fled to a detox center, followed by thirty days at a treatment center. Looking back, I would have been ripe for intervention ten years earlier. One of my deep regrets is that these formal interventions are a recent phenomenon. I would have dearly loved being the center of attention at my very own intervention—the attention I had craved so since childhood.

Since I had known fifteen years beforehand that I was an alcoholic, going to AA was not difficult for me at first. I could easily say, "I'm an alcoholic." I knew that for years. Only gradually did my thinking evolve to where the meetings were making me feel more uncomfortable than fulfilled. After twenty-seven years of heavy smoking, too, my use of cigarettes and caffeine increased greatly, as I transferred addictions. Other abuses were sprouting, too.

Frequently all it required to turn accepting "serene" AA-program people into raging adversaries was the innocent inquiry, "Why must we close with the Lord's Prayer?" [My] desperate need for approval forced me to compromise my beliefs and endure the animosity that followed such questions. In the very beginning, the rigidity of the group was helpful, but that same rigidity years later was equally harmful. Something snapped in me when I asked at a women's AA meeting, "If we are perceived by the public, the 'normies,' to be a religious organization, which we may not be, but if we're perceived to be that, why must we close with the Lord's Prayer? What if that keeps just one woman out there suffering and even dying as a result?" And this woman, this accepting inventory-taking woman, said to me, "So let her die." Something snapped when I heard that. It was at this time, coincidentally, that I read an announcement in *Free Inquiry* about Secular Organizations for Sobriety—SOS—and my life hasn't been the same since.

Another woman and I started an SOS group in our city. What I like is that at SOS, the program is different for someone with seven years of sobriety than for someone with seven weeks. It expands, and original thoughts are not stomped on. I do think we succeed in being nonjudgmental in our group. Instead of being told that we're nothing—that we're just a step away from a drink, whether we have seven years or seven weeks of sobriety—we're told that we're terrific, that we're wonderful. This is so necessary, especially for women who have had low self-esteem. We don't need a program designed to create humility when we cannot think of one good thing to say about ourselves, because we're drinking women. I never hear a dire warning at SOS meetings to . . . "Beware of being happy, because you're going to *pay* for that happiness."

Drinking is no longer an option or an attraction for me. I drank too hard for too long with too much suffering. If I had only forty-eight hours to live, I still wouldn't want to pour a drink. . . . (I gave up smoking over three years ago)—but, like the song says, "Don't give me that line."

Sam: Thank you, Emma, for pointing out how important self-esteem is for sobriety.

Your turn, Don.

Don: I'm Don, 55, with over five years' sobriety. Well, I have two brothers—one older—and one younger sister. Best I can re-call, it was your usual Beaver Cleaver–type All-American child-hood, no complaints whatsoever. We were all provided for as best my father could manage. We didn't do without an awful lot of things. The bikes that we got weren't always new but we always had bikes, we always had ball gloves, we always had the middle-class trappings. We ate well. I was quite content.

I was a real straight arrow—very high moral and ethical standards—and probably was a model teenager. It wasn't until I got into college and had my first experience with alcohol that I started to act up and misbehave. I imagine that alcoholic drink-ing started at that particular time. Of course I was totally unaware of it and never really got into serious trouble. In college I first developed a very strong suspicion and dislike for authority fig-ures, which carried through into the Army, where I was very un-happy. Did a lot of drinking there. It's all I could think of to do to occupy my time. Even though there were other outlets, nothing else occurred to me, and drinking is what I enjoyed.

The first job I had, of any significance, on getting out of the Army—I was about 23–24—was with a large corporation. I was on the road. It was a relatively unstructured job—I could determine what hours were the optimum hours to work. This just gave me more opportunity and more freedom to drink. There was no office to report to on a regular basis, no time clock to punch, and driving around in different areas I found it opportune to stop in for a beer at various times. Every evening I'd drop by a local pub to meet friends and hang around and drink some more. It's about all I did really. I didn't have any leisure activities. Being single, I wasn't into any sort of household repairs or anything like that. This continued on until '64, when I got married, and, even then, I just continued with the drinking. I thought one of the wonderful features of getting married and having my own residence—an apartment of my own—was the fact that I could now stock the refrigerator with beer. And it just seemed to permeate every aspect of my life. I didn't miss an opportunity to partake.

My wife was upset even at that time, thinking that I drank too much, or there must be some things that we could engage in that didn't involve drinking, but my opinion at that time— and for many many years—was if it didn't involve drinking it wasn't worthwhile doing. Mind you, I wasn't always drunk, but I generally had a buzz on, or was working on one, or trying to get one. Very seldom could I be seen without a beer in my hand.

We relocated, met new friends, and those that I chose to get close to were those who enjoyed the same leisure activity: drinking, hanging around barrooms after work, going to bars for lunch hour. It never really interfered with my job, which is one of the things that blinded me to the fact that I had a problem. As long as I was productive—and I was—I just didn't see it as a problem. I don't know how long we had been married when my wife initially started harping on this: I drank too much, I drank so much more than all of my friends. I just couldn't see it. If I did, it was because they chose to drink less than I did. Mine was normal drinking, and others, just for their own particular motivation or reasons, chose to drink less. But I certainly wasn't experiencing any problem.

We had one child of our own, adopted another one. I was a good father, really enjoyed the company of my kids, spent a lot of time with them. The drinking certainly didn't abate to any appreciable degree. It just kind of plateaued out at steady consumption. [I] still didn't think I had much of a problem—until I experienced an unexpected loss of employment, totally unrelated to any alcohol consumption. . . .

I actually began to feel myself that I might really have a serious problem during the period I had the best job of my career, and the best job in my experience. I enjoyed what I was doing, I was paid well, nice benefits, particularly an expense account, and I was on the road constantly, and found that every single night I was in a bar, in a motel, drinking. Nothing but drinking. Never saw a movie. Never tried to find out if there were a sports event in town. Just drinking. And it was getting totally out of hand. I began to think then that I might want to try to tone it down a little bit, try to get a grip on it. Before I had an opportunity to do this, the job was pulled out from under me, and this had nothing to do with drinking. And it was during this period of unemployment, with the bills closing in, and unable to find a job during the recession in '80 and '81 that the drinking really picked up. And it was causing considerable problems around the house.

The drinking had really accelerated, particularly around the house. I was becoming embarrassed over the condition I found myself in, never planning to get in that condition, but finding myself inebriated, *obviously* inebriated, or terribly, terribly hung over in the presence of my kids. The economic situation was such that we had to sell the house. My wife and the kids went to the West Coast and, at the time, I thought, at the urging of my friends, about the only place I could hope to find decent employment, or any sort of a job, would be in Texas. At the time, during the recession, it had the only glimmer of thriving economy.

But I found myself down there with *all* the restraints removed— all the support systems of family and friends gone, totally on my own, in a strange town. I just went bonkers. Not just being in the bars every night, but many times during the afternoon. I had a job that I could see was going to go absolutely no place. It was doomed to self-destruct. The drinking fed on my depression, and the depression fed on my drinking. I first began to encounter the symptoms of severe withdrawal. I used to get the shakes to such a degree that I was unable to sign my name on a check. My physical condition deteriorated rapidly. I was frequently jaundiced; had the shakes.

I first made an effort to stop by going to AA, and met with some initial success. I lasted about three months, I guess, and I attribute the success due to my elation over my having apparently gained control over the problem. But I could not handle or get a grip on the AA philosophy—it just seemed totally illogical to me. I also found that the network of friends that I had were all barroom- and drinking-centered friendships. To maintain the friendships I found myself back in the bars again, initially drinking club soda or Coke or coffee, but it was just a question of time before I broke down one night and just said, "What the hell? Everybody else is having fun. I'm not—not the extent I used to, and I know what the missing ingredient is." So I just had a series of relapses, over and over and over again.

The slips or relapses were not periods of short duration. I'd go back to drinking and I'd generally last five or six months, sometimes longer, until I just got in the state of total physical and psychological deterioration and would go back to AA again, this time determined to stick it out and try to grasp the mysteries of the program. Invariably, after continued exposure, I'd just come to the conclusion that if indeed this was the secret, or the only method, to achieve permanent sobriety, that I was doomed to failure, because I simply could not accept any of it. Since it was presented as the only thing that did work or could work, and I knew it wouldn't work for me, the logical conclusion was I'd better go back to what I do best, which was drinking.

It continued on that way—on again, off again. My employment situation was getting increasingly worse, to a point where I found myself just able to work day to day. The [national] financial collapse was so severe that I couldn't get any sort of a job, but I was not alone there. I finally returned to upstate New York, where I took an alcohol rehab, and found it to be a major disappointment in that it was nothing or little more than institutionalized AA, under federal government auspices. But since I was a guest in my younger brother's home, I endured a period of about five months of enforced sobriety, and I rankled under it, but I didn't have the heart to disappoint him and his family by drinking in their presence.

I left his area to return to my hometown, thinking that my employment opportunities would be better. Once I found myself on my own again, I resumed the drinking. After a period of about six months, I came to the conclusion that there was no possible way I could ever handle it again, normally. I was on an extremely restricted income and still found that I was spending the bulk of my money on alcohol. It wasn't working, and I was barely working, and it was taking its toll on me.

I went to AA again and got a grip on it. I was able to stop but found myself, after a period of about six months—the longest period of sobriety I had obtained up to that point—totally disenchanted with the program. I found myself going primarily to socialize and to avoid finding myself with extended periods of solitude. I knew it wasn't good for me to be totally by myself, and I knew no harm would come to me going to an AA meeting. But with increased sobriety came increased disillusionment with the entire program. I just wrote it all off as something to be endured rather than a learning situation. And finally I just couldn't stomach anymore—I have a low BS tolerance—and decided that I would divorce myself from any activities. The price that I felt I had to pay for a few minutes of socialization just wasn't worth it. I just stopped attending meetings altogether and did a lone-wolf sobriety for a year and a half, going on two years—totally on my own. But I felt I had a grip on it: one of my primary motivations in remaining sober was in taking perverse delight in not falling victim to the AA members' predictions that failure to attend regular meetings would inevitably result in a relapse and that I would start drinking again. So I just stayed sober primarily to prove them wrong.

It worked. I didn't feel as if I were coming unhinged in any way whatsoever, but I also missed a social connection. I missed some support but felt under no circumstances was it worthwhile going back again. If anything, listening to the ever-so-predictable monologues and the like, I found it so depressing that I was actually more tempted to drink after attending one of those meetings. I thought, My God, if this is sobriety, boozing never looked so good!

I then read in the newspaper about SOS, and out of curiosity decided to attend my first meeting, which was very sparsely attended. My initial reaction was, "Where were you when I could have used you?" But when I saw that it was so sparsely attended, I felt a moral or ethical obligation to, if nothing else, just lend my physical presence to the SOS group, to give it some degree of validity. I could think of nothing worse than someone who had never tried a support group attending an SOS meeting, or attempting to, and finding a vacant room. So I started going, and the more I went, the more at ease I felt. . . . My views in AA were always met with considerable clucking and disfavor. The more I saw that dissenting views were tolerated in SOS—and indeed were viewed as intellectually stimulating, actually encouraged—the more at home I felt. I find it extremely stimulating. The field, or subject, of alcoholism is extremely important to me. I like to stay current. I like to read about the subject, about current views, research, and the like and find that many of the people at the meeting are conversant with divergent opinions and views. People do pay some regard and some respect to scientific studies being done within the current year, rather than deriving bizarre views from an antiquated book of some fifty years vintage.

I found it to be a rewarding experience. I don't feel dependent on it—a big plus, I think, for SOS. I don't feel I need it; I go because I enjoy it. I can *not* attend a meeting should anything else come up, without these portents of impending doom hanging over my head, [but] I haven't found too many things during the course of a normal week that I would consider to be of sufficient importance to take precedence over an SOS meeting. I just enjoy them: the company, the fellowship, the camaraderie, and, what I consider to be a refreshing, scientific, rational, a stimulating approach to the subject. Everyone is not in lock-step, and there is no attempt made to change opinions one way or the other. Everyone is entitled to his or her opinion. . . . There is nothing like it around, and I feel that there is a need for it. I feel that anyone attempting to quit, or recently obtaining some sobriety, and looking for a means to bolster their commitment, would find it extremely productive, would find it, hopefully, somewhat of an answer—if not the total answer—to their need for fellowship, for a support group. . . .

Sam: Gee, Don, I appreciate your sharing your experiences with SOS. Thanks for giving us all an idea of what SOS can be.

OK, Joan, we'd really like to hear from you now.

Joan: I'm Joan, and I'm 37 years old. I've been sober for four years. I was born in a small town on the Oregon coast. There were seven children in my family (I was number five): three boys, three girls, one boy. My father was a logger, and my mother later went to work after he had a logging accident. My little brother was severely burned. We had a series of family crises, but before that, my father was just a typical man of the times, I guess: You drink and you fight, and that was what he did. My father was pretty violent; my mother was passive, tried to keep the peace. A lot of criminality and unhealthy behaviors sprang out of that environment. [The] older brothers came of age during the late sixties and got into drugs. They've been into alcohol. Everybody was into alcohol where I came from: it was just a way of life, just something you assumed that people did. In those days we didn't diagnose a man who drank like today, like the recovery culture will diagnose anybody as an alcoholic. The way my father drank was just the way men drank in those days. And my mother —no one would talk about her as being an enabler; you're a wife, a floozy, or a barfly, and that was about it. There was really no terminology or thought of supporting an alcoholic, or other kinds of mythology or beliefs that we have about alcoholism today.

I was pretty resistant to a lot of things that went on. I did the same thing when it came to drinking that everybody else did: I started about 12 years old. We'd drink three beers, throw up, and that was it. We were drunk after that. We didn't drink anymore. We didn't have any more. If we did, that was a limit. My sisters and I did that; we'd sneak out and do whatever we had to do to have a good time: hitchhike to town, go fifteen miles and just drink with our friends every weekend. When weed came around, I smoked weed. I did not get stoned, so I didn't smoke weed. I didn't really get into that until I was about 23. . . .

I don't consider myself technically an alcoholic. I don't even like the term. I like to consider myself a person who chooses not to drink and not to use. I was habituated to both alcohol and marijuana for about fifteen years. I primarily used those things to cope and, of course, I got physiologically hooked into the cycle, and I used them to cope with my own enablement strategies. Being a middle child, I assumed the family hero role. I needed to cope, and that was my way of coping. When I dropped drugs and alcohol, I also dropped the enmeshment in the family. I'm a writer also, writing some self-help–type books, fiction, and other things.

I didn't even go to AA. For the first nine months I just dropped weed, cigarettes, and alcohol on the same day, just prior to Christmas. I did not go to any groups or organizations—I just drifted along. I finally realized that the family system [had] kind of hooked me back in. So many things were escalating and I was feeling the patterns happen again, and I started having using and drinking dreams. So I decided to go to Al-Anon. And I went into the Al-Anon programs, and I immediately reacted to their religious atmosphere. I fought the system, and it didn't work. But through that system I met someone who was into Adult Child of Alcoholics. I went to that group, and it was a little bit less,— the environment was less religious. It [met] in a house, and the slogans weren't posted all over the walls. They did some of the same things, but I didn't have as violent a reaction to it. I eased through that, and then I continued to have the using and drinking dreams, so I thought, "Well, I better do something before I go back to using and drinking." I went into AA and I fought that system all the way, and I began to see there's a big behavioral psychology system where they're inducing behavioral spiritualism in people. I have immense problems with that system.

I re-wrote the Lord's Prayer, and I called it a universal prayer. (I don't even like the word *prayer,* but I think of it in a different way). I tried to institute that in some of these systems. I did a number of things. One day I just could not take it anymore, so I dropped out of all programs.

Then I saw an ad for SOS in one of the community bulletins or something. So I went into the SOS group, and the way I see SOS, it is a collection of very independent people who are going to be, or [are] striving to be, *committed* to sobriety, and they're going to find it, they're going to have it, and they're going to keep it, no matter what they do. Before I got into SOS, I was reading a magazine, and I saw an ad for *How To Stay Sober: Recovery Without Religion,* and I [thought], "Oh my God!—Nobody in the world's ever thought of this before, apparently, because everyone's so into 12-Step groups." I read *Unhooked* and [felt] relief to realize that everybody is not brainwashed; everybody is not into this; and everyone doesn't just automatically go with this program: They say one thing, they do another.

My realization with AA was I had walked out of one very unhealthy family system and straight into another one. They had the same rules: "Don't talk; don't think; don't feel; don't notice what's going on." They say one thing, they do another. They claim that what they're actually saying and doing is not even happening. It's very confusing. There's an institutionalized denial in the AA program. So I got into SOS, and I found that there weren't really any problems there. You could do whatever you wanted. There's not a "big book" as such, in terms of their biblical form of the "Big Book" in Alcoholics Anonymous.

I found that the people in SOS are much more intellectual. We share ideas. There are no topic controls. We can talk about any group, like those in AA can't. We freely share literature, ideas. Everyone brings in articles and exchanges things, and any time there's a new theory of alcoholism, or new theories related to family systems—whatever it is—we read it, we discuss it, we can be critical about it, and it's a much healthier, open system. It feels to me like people can have an impact in this system, within their group, and beyond their group. In AA you can fight the system for the rest of your life and never make any impact in that system, never change anything.

Sam: Thanks for highlighting the fact that our topics for discussion here at SOS are virtually unlimited. If you read a book or article, see a movie or play, or watch a TV show that is interesting to you, please feel free to share it with the group.

Norm, would you like to conclude?

Norm: I'm Norm, 34 years old and sober for two-and-two-thirds years. I grew up on the upper West Side of Manhattan during, I guess, until about 1972. We lived in a university neighborhood, where I went to public school and was very much influenced by the mood of the sixties, even though it wasn't quite [part of] my age group. I considered that drugs were to be sort of a naturalization into adulthood, along with radical politics, left-wing politics, etc., etc.—the myriad of Vietnam-era phenomena.

I began experimenting with drugs, I guess, when I was in the seventh grade—I began smoking marijuana; and I found it enjoyable and helped to break up the stress of living in the city. . . . So that was an escape for me. Later, when my family moved to the suburbs of New Jersey in 1972, I began to experiment with other drugs, such as LSD, and found that I could really tolerate being intoxicated on LSD on quite a regular basis. And I did some drinking in high school—not much heavily, because it was very hard to . . . actually it was easier for me to gain access to soft drugs than to alcohol. . . . I later found at some point that I wasn't able to take drugs and maintain my sensibilities, and I ended up doing a lot of time in mental institutions and psychiatric halfway houses. . . .

Somehow I managed to find my way to Boston, where I attended school. Unfortunately, my being predisposed toward using drugs led me to the use of cocaine. I became severely addicted to cocaine at a certain point in my twenties and experienced very difficult times because of that. In fact, I ended up finding one night that I had really called the police because I had had a paranoid psychosis due to the use of cocaine. The police were in my living room trying to figure out what was going on, and I was telling them I was just very beside myself, terrified that I had gotten that far that I actually had the police in my home trying to find where I had hidden the stash, and that I really had no idea what I was doing.

And so, the winter of 1989, I sought help and attended meetings of Narcotics Anonymous, where I found some strength to fight my battle against the cocaine, which I felt had attained a demonic control over my existence, so much so that I was willing to go along with anything NA told me. Everything they suggested that would help me fight the battle made sense to me at the time, because I really had no alternative until I found SOS in September of 1990.

At that time I realized I didn't have to fight my addictions in relation to any drug through fear; that you don't have to fight fear with fear; that I could stand up for myself and take credit for my sobriety, which at that point in time, I guess, was about a year and eight months, and that I could do this without surrendering my will to a higher power or a God.

Although I have a very cosmological view of the universe,

I didn't perceive God as the force or whatever have you that had caused me to become an addict. Therefore I didn't see it as God's responsibility to, as they say, remove the addiction. So I found myself much more comfortable in terms of what to me was the more reasonable approach that I found in SOS, where group support was not so much dependent on a kind of hierarchical structure of cliques. To give an example: At the end of an SOS meeting, we all go out for coffee together, whoever wants to go; whereas when I was working the program at Narcotics Anonymous, only certain people were asked—you had to be one of the right people, so to speak, to be asked to go out for coffee. If you hadn't attained a certain level of the 12 Steps, then you weren't asked to go out.

This social nexus was very important for me in SOS, and I find to this day that it really helps me keep in touch with what I center, in terms of my own sobriety. What it has become for me is something that I can do without having to terrorize myself into being sober and clean. So today sobriety means just being able to relax enough to realize that I don't have to use drugs or alcohol. At the same time I don't have to have the fear of God to experience that sobriety; and that no matter what happens, I really don't have to go off and do something for myself that I would regret. Basically everything is all right—the universe runs according to its own patterns, and we can all take credit for being clean and sober if we are, and [for] that I'm very grateful.

Sam: Norm, we all thank you for your concise, upbeat summary of your experiences and feelings about SOS.

I really enjoyed the opportunity to lead the meeting tonight. I realize that it has been unusually long, but it seemed important that we get to know each other at the outset. Future meetings should last only an hour and a half, including the coffee break; of course, you're free to leave at any time.

This meeting is self-supporting. If you can make some contribution, we will use it to help defray the cost of rent, refreshments, and other expenses. Norm, will you pass the basket around, please?

After the meeting, some of us go around the corner to the New Horizon Cafe on Porter and Dale. You are all invited and most welcome to join us there for some real coffee.

Sobriety is our priority, and we each assume the responsibility for our lives and our sobriety. Thank you for coming, and please come back. Let's close by giving ourselves a hand for being here to support and celebrate each other's sobriety.

Good night, be careful, and please join us again next week—we hope to see you here. Thanks again for coming.

The Forum*

___

*The opinions expressed in "The Forum" are those of the authors and do not necessarily reflect those of SOS or its members.

5. "The Fickle Gene": An Interview with Kenneth Blum

Richard Smith

The causes of alcoholism have perplexed me for some time. I wondered why the fickle finger of fate had pointed at me and said, "You will become an alcoholic." Was it because my father's father was born in Ireland? On the day after Christmas, 1990, I read that an article in the latest issue of the *Journal of the American Medical Association* (JAMA) questioned the validity of an April 1990 report linking alcoholism with the D2 receptor gene.

I read both articles and got the impression that the JAMA article, which had been written by Dr. David Goldman of the National Institute on Alcohol Abuse and Alcoholism (NIAAA), was sour grapes. It gave the impression of "It wasn't our research so it is not valid."

In the closing remarks of his April 1990 report, Dr. Kenneth Blum said: ". . . additional research is also required on living

Reprinted from the *SOS National Newsletter* 4, no. 3 (Fall 1991), and no. 4 (Winter 1991).

alcoholics and their relatives. In this respect, studies now in progress in our laboratory, using peripheral blood from large pedigrees, as well as from unrelated individuals of several different racial and ethnic groups, will further ascertain polymorphism of the dopamine D2 receptor gene or a gene close to the dopamine D2 receptor gene as a specific trait marker for alcoholism. . . . Further studies on the molecular genetics of alcoholism are needed as they could be of great benefit for the twenty-eight million American children of alcoholics who are potentially at risk for this disease."

An article in the Southwest Edition of the *Wall Street Journal* for July 15, 1991, "New Studies Lend Support to 'Alcoholism Gene' Finding" stated: "The initial report [by Dr. Blum] however was undermined in December when a government laboratory reported that it was unable to duplicate the finding. The new experiments support the initial finding, help explain why the second experiment was unsuccessful and, for the first time, implicate the genetic variation in a wider range of mental health disorders. . . . But the new reports appear to strengthen and clarify the first finding."

In one report scheduled for publication soon in the journal *Alcohol,* Drs. Blum and Noble searched for the A1 gene in DNA from the blood of 159 living people. They found the gene was present in 51 percent of alcoholics compared with 21 percent of nonalcoholics.

SOS founder Jim Christopher thought that other members of SOS might be interested in Dr. Blum's work and asked me to do a telephone interview with him and write an article about it. On June 3, 1991, I had the opportunity to do so.

SOS (Q): Why did you decide to hunt for an alcoholic gene? What got you started in this?

Dr. Blum (A): I think the way to explain that would be most interesting would be to go back early in my career. I received a bachelor's degree in pharmacy at Columbia University, and I was doing some research on the brain and what effects drugs have on it. I never really was a pharmacist; I just stayed in the laboratory. Then I moved out and eventually got a Ph.D. at New York Medical College in something called "neuropharmacology," which is the study of the effects of drugs on the nervous system. So, in my early formative years I became very interested in what was going on in the brain and how drugs affect the brain and can cause changes in behavior.

In 1967, I got involved with an old professor of mine in something called "psychopharmacology," which is the study of how drugs affect behavior. I worked with him and we got very involved with alcoholism. The reason was that the NIAAA came into being, and we applied for a grant looking at whether stress can induce drinking in animals as it does in humans. It sounded like an easy thing to do, but we found out when we put animals into stress conditions during the week they didn't drink, but on the weekends they did drink. This was strange to us, kind of like weekend binges, and I decided that the only difference was the environment, especially the lighting. We eventually decided to put rats in a dark closet to see if they would drink more, and lo and behold, the animals we put into a dark closet for two weeks drank like crazy. There is no noise, there is nothing stressful, it's kind of a relaxing spot to be in, and rats are nocturnal, so you would think that they could handle it; and they drank tremendously. What that did was give us a clue that there must be something going on in the brain chemically that induces some kind of craving behavior in animals.

From that particular experiment I realized that brain chemistry probably has more to do with uncontrollable drinking than the environment. So we spent the next twenty-two years studying how brain chemistry could, number one, affect drinking behavior; and, number two, how alcohol and drugs could affect brain chemistry, which would affect subsequent drinking; and number three, the effect of alcohol on future births, in terms of siblings of the next generation.

Q: You mean in relation to genes—the passing on of this trait.

A: That got us into things like transmitters, so that in the early stages we began to study transmitters that are involved in behavior, such as dopamine or serotonin. For example, serotonin is involved in causing sleep and dopamine is involved in causing hyperactivity. We began to look at and explore these transmitters and how they relate to the effects of alcohol and how alcohol relates to their content. In doing all this work, we began to realize we were getting nowhere in really understanding what makes an addict an addict. I mean, you can have them drink alcohol or take heroin or cocaine, and that doesn't really tell you why they are going to be using drugs and alcohol. We thought there must be something that predates the use—something in the brain that was, in our opinion, going to be genetic.

In the seventies, there were lots of studies, as you know, that went on, with the Swedish, the Danish studies, and the work of Goodwin, suggesting that if, for example, you had a biological parent who was an alcoholic, that was more important than your environment as to whether you would become an alcoholic. If you are a male and either your mother or your father was an alcoholic, you have four times the risk of becoming an alcoholic than the general population, independent of your environment. If you are a female, you have a three times higher risk.

These studies were the beginning of people thinking about whether genetics was what we call antecedent to alcoholism. Having been in the field since the seventies, one thing I really wanted to do was understand what craving behavior was all about. I knew it had to do with transmitters. I didn't know which ones, but I knew it had to do with brain chemistry. Way back in 1959, Gerald McLearn bred a strain of mice that hated alcohol and another strain that loved it. Now that we have these two strains of mice, we can study them to see if the brain chemistry is different. At about this time it was found that opiate peptides—natural opiates—are found in the brain. They are generally called endorphins.

I decided to look into the brains of these genetically bred

animals, and found a clear-cut difference in the animals that loved to drink alcohol. They had a very low amount of endorphins compared with the animals that did not like alcohol. So I thought then that one of the genetic elements in causing alcoholism or maybe even drug dependence was a low level of endorphins. That was the first clue that we thought that we had for genetic evidence that drinking was tied to some biochemical abnormality in the brain. This then led us to explore some avenues in which we found that certain animals have lower serotonin levels. We found that other transmitters are different in genetic animals. This gave us a feeling that these neurochemicals in the brain may be defective, and that there is a place in the brain that is called the reward center, and that there are all these transmitters that work in one area of the brain. This area of the brain is involved in feeling good, or pleasure states. If something goes haywire in the chemicals that, in a sense, mediate or provide a feeling-good response, then the person is going to be robbed of the chemistry that he or she needs to carry on a normal, happy, and healthy life. This is the area of the brain where we began to search for the clue to the genetic tendency to become an alcoholic. That was our blueprint.

That is where we began to explore. Each chemical controls behavior and each chemical is controlled by a series of genes and if something goes wrong with the genes that make these chemicals, we figured that people without the right stuff up in their brains would be more prone to use alcohol and drugs. I know some of these words may mean nothing to your readers, but does this make sense to you?

Q: It is a little tough to follow at times but I think I get it. . . . Would you like to discuss the fact that the Irish and Russians have a high incidence of alcoholism and that Jews and Orientals have a low incidence?

A: Now the national origins story is, I think, very important because it is what we call selective breeding.

Q: Okay, the same thing you did with the mice.

A: Right.

Q: You could duplicate these human traits in mice since they reproduce rapidly.

A: That is right. Ninety-seven percent of all Jews drink alcohol. But only .67 percent become alcoholics. On the other hand, you can have in the American Indian, let's say, 100 percent drink and 85 percent become alcoholic; they are much more prone. Now before we get into all the ethnic backgrounds, I would say that there is a sort of cruel logic of genes. For example, Orientals, as you pointed out, have a low incidence. This is why. When an individual drinks alcohol, there is a way of breaking alcohol down to another substance called acetaldehyde. There is an enzyme called aldehyde dehydrogenase that takes the acetaldehyde and breaks it down to CO_2 and water. An example of a drug that is used in the alcohol field to prevent drinking is Antabuse. Antabuse prevents the enzyme aldehyde dehydrogenase from working, so it builds up as acetaldehyde as you drink—you have your Antabuse in there, so you're going to get deathly ill and get sick and faint or whatever, because the acetaldehyde is very toxic. Now it turns out that the Oriental has something like a built-in Antabuse. They do not have, genetically, enough aldehyde dehydrogenase to break down the acetaldehyde when they drink. They get a red-flush face. This genetic defect is a protective mechanism, so that Orientals cannot drink as much as they may want to.

I am told that about 40 percent of Orientals have this gene defect and that of the other 60 percent, half of them do a lot of drinking. So there is a cruel logic of genes.

On the other hand, there are genes that are not protective. There are genes that, for some, mutated and have clustered in various segments of society, and that is the gene that we think that we are talking about in our work: a gene that is mutated and a gene that is not a very happy gene.

Q: Certainly the results of having it are not happy for the people who have it.

Tell me about the gene that you found in the dopamine D2 receptor in the brains of alcoholics you studied.

A: What Dr. Noble and I did was take tissue from the brains of seventy deceased people in our study. Thirty-five were diagnosed as alcoholics and the other thirty-five had no alcohol problems. We took DNA out of these people and we matched a piece of the DNA that is defective with 69 percent of the people who died of alcoholism, and there was a very high percentage of people having a defective gene. Now it turns out, to understand it a little better, everybody has this gene. Everybody has D2 receptor genes. The only problem is you may have a fault in your D2 receptor gene. We see one form as a normal gene and the other form, we think, is an abnormal form. It turns out that in the general population, if you exclude alcoholism and other drugs—which is very important—then about 12 to 15 percent have the abnormal form. We see the normal form in 85 percent or more. What we found was that 69 percent of the people who died had the abnormal form.

Q: From your April 1990 article, I understand you found the gene on chromosome 11. Did you find anything else that would indicate that there is also another gene that would cause alcoholism? Also, in some people who had the abnormal gene but did not become alcoholics, is there another gene that might be suppressing and making them alcoholics?

A: Well, yes. There are all kinds of possibilities. Let's see if we can straighten that out.

One possibility is with individuals who have the A1 allele of the D2 receptor gene. Remember there are A1 and A2 alleles. Persons with the A1 allele of the D2 receptor gene may be at high risk to become severe alcoholics or drug abusers. It may be that people who have the A2 allele may not be at risk at all from all this, or it may be another gene we have not yet been able to identify that could still put them at risk for alcoholism.

In essence, we have found only the first gene that may in part be at risk for alcoholism or drug abuse. The third possibility is if you are an alcoholic, you may not have the A1 allele, but you may have another gene or some environmental factor that has nothing to do with genes that makes you an alcoholic.

Q: I understand that there are some studies that have traced twins from alcoholic parents. Often, even after being split up and put in separate foster homes, both twins become alcoholics, regardless of whether there was drinking in the new home.

A: I believe that. I also believe that if you had a hundred alcoholics lined up, my guess would be, based on some calculations, that 33 percent would be genetic [alcoholics] and the rest of them would be nongenetic. But here's the catch—when you go to a treatment center, the people that really need the help are mostly genetic types. You'll end up in the treatment center with about 90 percent being genetic in origin.

Q: That's interesting, because these are the type of people that you had the samples from; the ones with the very high percentage of faulty genes.

A: They can't control it. In other words, we're talking about people who have very high tolerance at birth to drink a lot of alcohol. They drink and can't stop. But they pass a point where they still get cirrhosis of the liver. They still can get intoxicated. They get dysphoric. They get to the point where they get ulcers and all kinds of other problems. But they are drinking tons of alcohol compared to the normal population. And they eventually get themselves into great trouble, such as difficulty with the law, or they end up in the treatment centers. Then they are on the road to probably many more relapses until they die of alcoholism.

Q: So really what you're saying is that of the thirty-three out of the hundred that you lined up against the wall, most of them are the ones that end up as really hard-core drinkers.

A: They're the ones that everybody is really worried about.

According to what America would call alcoholics (which is about four drinks a day) those people may or may not be true genetic alcohlics. But that doesn't mean that they have the right, that they should drink anyway.

Q: There was a comment on a local TV show in May about a new drug that was billed as a cure for alcoholics. In experiments with rats that loved alcohol, it reduced their desire to drink by 40 percent to 60 percent.

A: I don't know, I'm trying to think which one that was. But the thing is, when you talk about controlled drinking, there is no way that you can have controlled drinking if you are genetically prone. That is taboo.

Q: That is why we stress in all of the SOS literature about recovery that there is absolutely no drinking or using. Period. Or forget it. "Don't come here, we can't help you."

A: Right. Because what happens is you end up going back and you relapse. You start that cycle again. Your body, your genetic makeup, will not allow you to be without it because it wants it so badly that you need it. What we're really saying here is that in the genetic world in which genes are being discovered, we are talking about maybe a third of the alcoholic community, but it's the most important third that we consider.

Q: They are the ones who have the greatest problems.

A: Yes, and the other thing you mentioned about finding other genes. I would say yes, we're searching for the other genes and other markers, and some have been found and not been reported yet. I can't tell you what they are yet, but I can say that it looks like there will be multiple genetic causes. Some more work will verify that soon. It is getting very exciting because some people may have one "bad" or defective gene while somebody else has two defective genes.

Q: If you happen to have two or more defective genes, then the chances are greater that you will be an alcoholic?

A: If you have only one you may be part of the 33 percent. These genes may be related to each other. This is an ongoing thing.

Q: Your original research was done with a DNA sample taken from brain tissue and you're now working with blood samples. Is that right?

A: Yes, there is a new report out in *Alcohol*—a very important journal in the field of alcoholism. This report with Dr. Ernest Noble of UCLA confirms our work by showing that when we separate less severe from severe, 60 percent of the severe alcoholics have this form. This report was published in the October 1991 issue. I want to mention another thing. People have to realize that alcoholism and drug abuse are compulsive diseases.

Q: That is an excellent point. I agree completely that all of us who are alcoholics have a compulsive nature; I know that I do.

A: At this point, we think there are at least six subsets of compulsive disease. One is helplessness, the feeling that you can't win. Another is high stress levels. The others are anger, aggressiveness, impulsiveness, and craving. These are the subsets of compulsive disease; alcohol and drug abuse are just manifestations that account for the craving.

Q: Would overeaters fall into this category?

A: Yes. There are overeaters who are carbohydrate bingers who fall into this category, but not fat and protein lovers, sugar bingers, or chocoholics. If an overeater likes fat and protein more than carbohydrates, I don't think they're chemical. I don't think they fall into the same compulsive disease.

Q: As I understand it, then, if overeaters like fat and protein, they may have emotional or some other problem that makes them overeat.

A: Yes, and there are those people who can't metabolize fat well. That's another gene.

Q: We spoke earlier about your needing people to send you blood samples for your ongoing research. Are there any special types of people you need?

A: We particularly need nonalcoholic blacks, but nonalcoholics probably are not going to read your newsletter. We are also looking for children of alcoholics. There is another very important factor I think is very interesting—something called psychosomatic.

Q: Yes, of course.

A: I have a new idea. It's called somatopsychic, which means the opposite. You are born with some cellular structural damage in the brain. That leads to some behavioral changes at birth, so that it's the genetic change of brain chemistry affecting these cells in your brain. That's somatic, and can lead to somatopsychic tendencies.

Q: I think I understand it.

A: In that group of mental illnesses, there are probably three types. One is something that you know as affective disorders, which include depression and bipolar manic-depression. Another is compulsivity. You don't have to be psychotic to drink alcohol. That's not the only reason you drink alcohol. You don't have to be a depressive to drink alcohol. You can be compulsive and have certain characteristics, etiologies, that make it a primary disease. People can be born with a primary disease characterized as compulsivity. They don't have to be manic-depressive or psychotic to have that other disease. Now if you are psychotic and happen to be manic-depressive, you can drink anyway. They do interrelate. But to have each component (these three components that I told you about) under the umbrella of somatopsychic syndrome has its own etiologies and you don't have to be one or the other, but you can have more than one problem. Do you understand what I am saying?

That's very important, because people have got to realize that the whole idea of a support group is that you get people who are coming in because they are manic-depressives and they are drinking. You get people coming in because they are schizophrenic and they are drinking. And there are people who come in who are purely compulsive.

Q: Right. They end up in the same place—they all end up being alcoholics.

A: Yes, but you may have to treat the manic-depressives with lithium or tricyclics, as well as treating their alcohol and drug problems with other drugs.

Q: I think we have covered just about everything. Is there anything else you want to add?

A: The only thing we did not cover is that people really want to know what can be done about alcoholism.

Q: That sounds interesting. Perhaps we could do an interview about that in the future.

A: We could go through some treatment approaches. We have developed some amino acids, nutritional therapy, and natural alternatives. Not taking drugs, but natural ways—vitamins and other nutrients that seem really helpful in taking the edge off. Focusing people into recovery, that's important.

Q: That sounds interesting. Let's plan on doing another interview soon.

*   *   *

In January of 1991, I wrote to Dr. Blum, telling how much I enjoyed his article. I said I was interested and concerned about the gene theory because I had five children and eight grandchildren. Had I passed on "the bad seed"?

In late January, I was invited to have myself, my children, and grandchildren become involved in the ongoing research into the gene theory.

Small samples of my blood and that of some of my children and grandchildren have been sent to Dr. Blum. I hope that all of my family will eventually become involved in the study.

If any readers would like more information about donating blood to this gene research, contact Dr. Kenneth Blum at The University of Texas Health Service Center at San Antonio, 7703 Floyd Curl Drive, San Antonio, TX 78284-7764, or call (512) 567-4225.

6. An Essay by an Escapee from Recovery Cultism to an Empowerment System

Susan E. Smith

A new myth is taking shape and form in the recovery market-place. The rumor of an Anti-Recovery Movement is stirring the blood of the "Keep It Simple" crowd. As the damned and spiritually diseased throngs search the crowded streets for experience, strength, and hope, neurotic caregivers, ideologically overinvested sponsors, dogmatic authors, and mental health professionals promoting "one way" recovery spring up like groundhogs when the sun shines. The winds of denial blow hot as new diagnostic labels and translogical explanations—diseasing even dissent—multiply in the upper echelons of the Adult Children. Fear and paranoia trickle down through the ranks. Burning bushes speak and smoke rolls off the tongues of 12-Step Trekkies.

If there is any "anti-recovery" action, it is the neurotic compulsion to label and explain away the infusion of reason and choices into the recovery culture. The growth of alternative sobriety groups and the increasing numbers of former 12-Steppers deprogramming by liberated expression is not anti-recovery. It is no more anti-recovery to analyze sobriety systems than it is anti-love to analyze family systems. No backlash threatens the trend to chemical and emotional sobriety in this country. All we're seeing now is the inevitable fallout from the domination of the 12-Step institution as the one true road to recovery. The phrase "YOU MUST CHOOSE A HIGHER POWER" has assumed hypnotic qualities. Fast-talking 12-Steppers will tell you it can be anything from "a tree, a rock, to the power running through your computer." A few years ago Steppers claimed your Higher Power could be "a chair, the group, a doorknob, or a hairbrush." I could have sworn they knew me from high school. My Higher Power was a hairbrush.

It must be recognized that not everyone can be converted or silenced. Many of us no longer believe our silence is for the greater good, and any program is better than no program. There are other programs; alternatives created or sought by skeptics out of need and desperation because we found the 12-step organizations resistant to change. Individuals asking questions and expressing needs for adaptation are not threatening to a healthy group or system. Escapees from recovery cultism are not long past these stages. We grew tired of resistance and denial and ran away as fast as intellect would take us. And this is unfortunate, because controversy and change is not threatening, it is part of the process of expansion.

As the recovery movement experiences this expansion, the spiritualistic factions will grow stronger through reacting, evaluating, and adjusting to losing their monopoly on our nation's sobriety and recovery consciousness. Other methods of recovery will become more visible and available to the millions of people who value the sobriety they have maintained, or want to get sober and stay sober in good company.

Secular Organizations for Sobriety is one of those "other" groups, an alternative organization with a premise so simple and direct it's naturally confrontational to those who encourage and affirm transference from one dependency to another without a break in the action.

Our premise is the Sobriety Priority. We do not drink or use no matter what. We don't have any slogans or mythical hyperbole claiming unfounded success rates or kicking in salvation, spiritual awakening, or enlightenment with the deal.

SOS does not set up impossible conditions. We won't insist that you haven't healed your addiction until some invisible event occurs, like a "spiritual awakening." (Just try to figure that one out.) All we do in SOS is quit drinking and using. The intrinsic value and healing of sobriety is an awakening in itself. It creates room for deeper realizations, but the nature of those experiences is defined by you, and not the organization. Vague terminologies like "spiritual awakening" and "dry drunk" are effective control devices and finger-pointing strategies. SOS has no built-in one-upmanship methods. The program is straightforward and unambiguous.

We don't have to warn members to "Keep It Simple" to bypass the critical mind, override the contradictions in the program, and proceed directly to ideological hypnosis. SOS really is a simple organization without hidden agendas. All we promote is that the individual can take responsibility for the series of conscious decisions required to either use or not use. We don't encourage people to believe that unconscious processes or faulty spiritual connections trigger robotlike compulsions to drink or use. The unconscious mind may be an unlimited repository of everything from memories of birth trauma to knowing all the words to the theme from "Gilligan's Island," but it has no power over our elbow joints.

SOS has a direct meeting format. We reinforce the Sobriety Priority, offer support to new members, mention the library, and have announcements. After the weekly group leader opens the meeting and suggests a topic, it's truly an open forum. We don't have "tag" meetings where only the most fervent followers get picked. We don't take numbers and let spirits run the meeting.

We take no weekly vows of silence in the public domain. We are not sworn to anonymity, but we respect and honor anonymity as a matter of civilized discretion and courtesy.

SOS is a supportive and informative organization. We don't engage in hypnotic readings approved by headquarters that moralize about our "character defects." We don't send nonbelievers marching toward the perdition of "jails, institutions, or death." We don't believe our problems are caused by a mutating spiritual virus that compels us to lumber through life trapped in a one-act play entitled *No Exit without Spirit Guides*. We don't believe all our mistakes are directly related to a multigenerationally transmitted tragedy we've been condemned to repeat.

Most of us understand the interactive effects of socialization, family systems, physiological and emotional processes. We are coming to terms with the impacts of these factors on our growth and development. We acknowledge multiple causations for various problems in our lives, but the responsibility for change rests with us once we know what happened.

We don't avoid family systems issues or expressions of emotions and self-disclosure; but it is not our custom to engage in rambling drunkalogues, drugalogues, or foodalogues. We don't routinely strip down and wallow in regret or failure orgies to remind ourselves of where we've been and orient ourselves to where we are now. We don't have any dewy-eyed zealots or "oldtimers" to tell us how to work the program. No one is compelled to identify themselves by their former use patterns or neurotic status. We're just who we are, and if we happen to feel like identifying with our former behaviors we do, if not we don't.

Many of us feel the Sobriety Priority is enough to remind us of our commitment. We don't feel it's necessary or productive to attach labels on ourselves that must hang like millstones around our necks for life. We're sober and committed. We don't drink or use no matter what. We're finished with that chapter in our lives.

SOS is not a coercive or compulsive organization. There is

no position or belief system that overrides the stated purpose of the organization. SOS is honest. It says what it means and means what it says. You won't wake up one day and find yourself subordinate to an ideology, an institution, a "group consciousness," or a religion in denial.

We have no restrictions on topics, readings, or opinions. We are people who show up armed with information. When the current facts and issues are on the table we discuss our personal reasons for choosing what we accept and what we reject. Our reasons are sometimes subjective as well as rational. We are a collection of individuals in a creative, open, and growing organization, expressing the balance and growth within ourselves to the best of our abilities.

No sacred cows are safe, no information is withheld or suppressed, all opinions are welcome. One gray area seems to need frequent negotiation: the assumption that all members are atheists. It is often forgotten or overlooked that many people who end up in SOS are not atheists. We are primarily individuals who prefer to take responsibility for rational choices. We do not believe that spiritual viruses or unconscious compulsions cause everything from alcoholism to excessive shopping. We often have to determine where lines are drawn between expressing our opinions and beliefs in meetings and abusing others with our beliefs. There is no difference between having members of a spiritual group insist that "YOU MUST CHOOSE A HIGHER POWER," and members of a secular group saying "THERE IS NO GOD." Being neither a theist nor an atheist, the "God" and "no God" arguments have no bearing on my reasons for being a member of a secular sobriety group. I suspect there are many like me.

SOS is an organization that provides balance and choice in the recovery movement. Maintaining internal balance on secularism will keep the door open. We are open to anyone seeking sobriety in an inebriated society . . . a society drunk on diagnosis, pathologizing, revivalism, homeopathic spiritualism (and almost incidentally now), alcohol and other drugs.

Rampant pathologizing is toxic to many of us who know the difference between a disease and a behavior. Some of us call alcoholism a disease because chemical addiction occurs on the cellular level. Others don't even identify with that because we feel the series of decisions or behaviors required to activate cellular addiction are processes of the mind and emotions.

Alcoholism as a "disease" is not an institutionalized definition handed down by the founder of SOS, but James Christopher argues that, all the emotional and environmental factors aside, cellular addiction can occur spontaneously or with long-term use. It's probably absurd to relate alcoholism to family history. I'd like to meet someone who can prove no one drank in the long line of immigrants propagating down through the Welsh, Scottish, British, English, Germans, Italians, and Irish from which the majority of Americans descend. The Native Americans were exposed to alcohol by the settlers, but psychoactive drugs were used in religious rites. Omitting other races is not alcoholic ethnocentricism —how many cultures haven't discovered alcohol, stimulants, or narcotics in some form?

Encouraging people to affirm and believe in powerlessness, with surrender to spirits as the only way out, is propaganda. Before AA became a mainstream organization no one paid much attention to the evangelical elements of the movement. But shortly after Stanton Peele and Archie Brodsky wrote *Love and Addiction* in the seventies, the idea of spiritual pathology took off. Ironically, Stanton Peele is now at the forefront of the anti-pathology and powerlessness movement. His original intent was to show that relationship dependencies can be as confining as chemical addictions. He never said that a mutating spiritual virus was on the loose and no one was safe. That's where 12-step theorists and Adult Children entered as "caring nurturers," suddenly qualified to define and diagnose new diseases just as fast as the presses could print their books. Then counselors, educators, psychologists, and other mental health professionals jumped on the bandwagon.

Pathologizing nearly every aspect of the human condition has seeped into every crack in modern cultural consciousness.

And this process is not new: protective and projective mythologies have always multiplied around chaos. Even though there has been much research, our scientific understanding of human psychology, physiology, and chemical addiction is still in the Dark Ages.

The word "disease" has been used so loosely in the last few years that it's either meaningless or it describes everything people do, think, or feel. For all that we don't know about chemical addiction, one thing we do know. If it is actually a disease, it's the only common disease known that is completely arrested or totally preventable by not adding a substance to the body chemistry.

Despite interesting theories that "crisis junkies" or "thrill seekers" become addicted to their own brain chemicals, not enough is known to prove such connections. Another new concept to explain addiction is that people from dysfunctional families have over- or underactive chemical receptors in their brains from love deprivation or exposure to violence; therefore, they are predisposed to addiction and compulsive behaviors. It is beyond me why anyone would find comfort in the idea that they have brain damage because they were raised in a dysfunctional family. It is only in the most severely deprived conditions, usually involving starvation, that compromised brain development has been shown to occur. The rest of us have probably all experienced some degree of trauma and deprivation, but our brains probably function within normal ranges. Long-term alcohol and drug abuse can result in irreversible brain and organ damage, but if use is curtailed in time, damages are reversible.

Both science and spiritualism can be insidiously moral and coercive to "out-of-control" theories. If people seeking sobriety by choice begin to identify with unfounded "compromised brain development" theories, we will have affirmed another means of promoting powerlessness propaganda before results or research confirms such a notion.

Cellular addiction and habituation to alcohol and other drugs occur on the chemical level. Add chemicals to a system already predisposed to addiction by any number of factors, or regularly assault a fairly resistant system with chemicals, and physiological functioning will be altered. What occurs could be termed addiction, and in other cases it may be habituation. The process may be sudden or slow, but both habituation and spontaneous addiction can have devastating consequences or just compromise the quality of life. That compromise is enough to convince many people to choose sobriety. SOS is an organization that makes room for people who have decided to choose sobriety without having to reach late-stage alcoholism or even to "hit the bottom." We don't feel recognizing sobriety as a choice trivializes the seriousness of chemical abuse; it emphasizes our commitment. The national cost of alcohol and drug use to our country is in the billions. We're people who no longer want to be part of the problem, whether we have hit bottom or had a crisis of clarity, which is how I define my decision to choose sobriety.

You've undoubtedly heard of "toxic parenting," and toxic shame has practically become a household word in the last few years. Toxic shame is based on the premise that all of us were separated from our authenticity by shaming child-rearing methods. The theory is based on the idea that we lost contact with our true emotions in the prelogical stages of development. Before about the age of seven, we did not have the ability to differentiate between who and what we were and what happened to us or what we did.

The process of socialization and ineffective parenting can do progressive damage to a human being. But how can these wounds be healed by identity transference to various out-of-control theories or other shaming identifications like spiritual diseases?

The foundation of the concept of "Toxic Recovery" is the observation that the pendulum has swung too far into unhealthy language and labels an obsession with obsessive themes. Before escaping from the oppressive "support" of the many manifestations of the AA programs, I wandered lost in the philosophical maze of neo-Calvinistic predestination reinforced by such unwieldy concepts as spiritual diseases, multigenerational—and even psychic—transmission of shame, abuse, and "issues." Transmission of issues and dysfunctionality is said to occur even in the absence of detectable abuse. For example, I was in a class where a college professor actually said, "By the way . . . if you even touch a child on the shoulder and *think* sexual thoughts, you have sexually abused that child." This kind of paranoia about child abuse, sexual abuse, and emotional abuse has reached levels of mass hysteria. We won't become more effective in preventing abuse by attempting to manipulate thought control; we'll just become more puritanical and guilt-ridden, which supposedly feeds the cycle of abuse. That's the only part I do believe without reservations.

And smoking out "codependency" in intimate relationships is another national compulsion. As we desperately try to recover from the shame we carry that actually belonged to a great-grandparent, monitor actions and motivations for "sick" attempts to attach ourselves to any moving target, and gather a list of neurotic titles that we will keep for life—which is a "recovery" strategy—is it any wonder that recovery eludes so many?

It cannot be denied that what we learned in our family systems shaped our personalities and determined some of our journey in life. Family secrets do have a way of growing in the dark and many themes are repeated. But it doesn't take a psychic, a psychologist, or a "caring nurturer" to figure out why these themes are repeated, and the reasons aren't limited to multigenerational transmission of issues confined to any particular family. The content of myths, great tragedies, great literature, and fairy tales of all cultures carries the themes. Sex, death, birth, family, food, incest, violence, murder, love, drunkenness and escapism, prosperity or poverty, greed, lies, truth, self-destruction and self-actualization are the themes of the human condition. Human consciousness is complex and many things occur that cannot be rationally explained, but a retrograde philosophy of a recovery-culture version of Calvinism does not enhance our social and personal evolutions.

It doesn't take an exceptionally keen mind to notice that the spiritual disease theory and the pedestrian adaptations of psychological systems such as the concept of multigenerational transmission are just new twists on the idea of original sin. We are born doomed to carry the shame of our parents, who carried the shame of their parents. Only benevolent spirits can save us from either bad spirits or lack of spirits, which is known as "spiritual bankruptcy."

The spiritual-disease, spiritual-cure theory has managed to get its sticky *and* slippery fingers into every institution of American society. The 12-step program has infiltrated legal, educational, and medical professions and even corporations. Chemical offenders are court-ordered into spiritualistic sobriety programs; educators on college and university levels teach and espouse the 12 steps; corporations channel chemical abusers into AA-based programs. This is not because it has been quantifiably determined that the program *does* work, but because supporters have permeated social institutions with the ideology that the program *might* work.

SOS doesn't pretend its program works miracles if you work the program. We learn to live our lives sober and miracles take care of themselves. Many of us in SOS are deprogramming from toxic recovery concepts and powerlessness and pathology propaganda. Some of us need time and space to put the entire process called "recovery" in perspective, in our personal lives and in the public domain. We're standing up and claiming our rights as American citizens, and we're justifiably angry that a religion in denial has convinced our social, legal, educational, and even corporate institutions that spiritual revivalism is the solution to alcohol and chemical abuse and dependency. We want equal time and informed consent. If courts are going to order sobriety programs, give all the options. If corporations are going to send employees to outpatient programs, don't prescribe one over another. If theories of chemical dependency and treatment are going to be taught at the college and university level, no program should be promoted but all should be taught.

If you have reached a saturation point with diseasing and diagnosis, need more flexibility and autonomy, while also needing the support and synergy generated by intelligent, independent, and competent adults who prioritize sobriety and freedom from other compulsions, SOS is the medium that allows for this freedom. Toxic recovery programs and theories are rigid, exploitative, and coercive. If you've had enough of solutions that become the problem before you know what happened, there are alternatives. There is an organization where principles are not more important than people, a true democracy with only one firm principle—the Sobriety Priority. If you need support and involvement in an organization that won't enforce institutionalized denial and compromise your principles, the doors are open at Secular Organizations for Sobriety.

7. An SOS Approach to Overeating

Rosalind Gold, Esq.

Most people think of SOS as a secular organization for alcoholics. I am a compulsive overeater and have struggled with a severe weight problem most of my adult life. Yet I have used SOS principles and gone from 196 to 110 pounds in 18 months. Even more importantly, I've maintained my current weight for over two years.

My problems with food started early. For as long as I can remember, it has been a magical source of comfort and enjoyment for me. As a child, I eagerly anticipated meals with my favorite dishes and, while eating, felt transported into a private, wondrous realm. Food gave me a high, and I turned to it in response to nearly every strong emotion. I ate to relieve tension, anger, and depression, as well as to celebrate and even just to break the boredom. Though I overate as a child, I did not develop a weight problem until adolescence, when I gained many pounds in a few years.

In college, I went on serious eating binges where I quickly

Reprinted from the *SOS National Newsletter* 4, no. 1 (Spring 1991).

stuffed myself with junk food. I swung between binge periods and months of strict dieting, entering the classic weight-loss yoyo. I would lose some weight, then put it all back on and gain even more, then shed further pounds, then regain them. In the five years before joining SOS, I had yoyoed up to almost 200 pounds —quite obese for a 5'2" woman.

I felt horribly disgusted with myself for being so fat, but I was even more frightened by feeling that I was completely out of control. I felt I could not stop eating until I was totally stuffed. I often could not fall asleep unless I had binged before going to bed and was nearly sick to my stomach. I was going to great lengths to hide my binges from my family and friends. I often bought bags full of drive-in fast foods and binged on them in the car. I then threw away the wrappers and frantically tried to air out the car so my husband wouldn't discover what I'd done.

My 12-Step Experience

Before SOS, I had achieved my most sustained weight loss in a 12-step program for overeaters. The program exhilarated me at first. I loved the group support. For the first time in my life, I was talking with people who had done the same crazy things with food that I had. It helped relieve the shame and isolation. I also found that calling group members when things got bad was very helpful.

However, because I never believed in a higher power who could take responsibility for my recovery, I grew more and more disenchanted with the 12-step approach. Yet I was always too frightened to voice my true feelings, especially when members told me that doubting the higher power showed vanity, ego, and denial of my problem. I often heard that it wasn't enough to eat sensibly, lose weight, and rely on group support. If I didn't somehow complete this mysterious journey through the 12 steps, I would return to overeating. Because I was both frightened and grateful, I tried to play along, but after a while, I began to feel fraudulent and ashamed. I also wearied of the mental calisthenics of translating 12-step jargon into concepts that I could accept. Eventually, I stopped attending OA (Overeaters' Anonymous) meetings and regained all the weight I had lost.

When I heard about SOS over two years ago, I was desperate. The 12-step program had aided me temporarily, but I could not imagine pretending again that a spiritual approach would lead me to recovery. Yet I knew I needed help. I attended a Los Angeles SOS meeting, and though the other members were primarily alcoholics or drug abusers, they said a lot that was important.

SOS for Overeaters

Since then, I've used SOS principles in my own recovery (adjusting them here and there to address the differences between alcohol and food problems). For example, I believe that I must acknowledge that I am a compulsive overeater. I must accept the fact that I have a food problem—whether genetic, physical, psychological, or some mixture of all of them—and I must change my eating and lifestyle to keep myself from bingeing, weight gain, and poor health.

Through hard experience, I've come to believe that my overeating could threaten my life. I could slowly kill myself with health problems from the yoyoing weight gain and pernicious junk-food diet of compulsive overeating.

I also separate my eating and behavior program—my "abstinence"—from all other issues in my life. I don't use food to deal with my emotions, and I don't use problems as an excuse for overeating.

I've also found that the SOS emphasis on rational, critical thinking and individual responsibility is especially helpful for overeaters. Overeaters have a different relation to food than alcoholics do to alcohol. Alcoholics must make One Big Decision—not to drink. But overeaters, like everyone else, must eat to survive. At least three or four times every day, we must make decisions about food, and we must choose when, where, what, and how much to eat. It is therefore crucial that overeaters learn sound, responsible decisionmaking. Surrendering these choices to a higher power may be one of the worst things an overeater can do.

Instead, to create my program of recovery, I critically assessed the different approaches to nutrition and behavior modification. I also looked to my own experience. Overeaters are diverse. For instance, we often have trouble with different kinds of foods. I usually binged on greasy, fried food, but many others may tend to sugary foods or foods with white flour. Given the complexities of the situation and the puzzles of human metabolism, one person's ideal program may be another's iron maiden.

I developed an approach that has succeeded for me. It involves

- A low-fat, high complex-carbohydrate diet.
- Avoidance of foods that triggered binges in the past.
- Behavioral techniques that help me recognize when I have just satisfied my physiological hunger, and when my desire to eat is emotional rather than physical.
- Planning ahead, so I have time to prepare meals that fit in with my food program.
- Weighing and measuring my food occasionally, so I know how much I'm eating.
- Exercise. Bike riding, jogging, and weightlifting have been crucial to my recovery. They not only burn calories, but in addition kill appetite. They also vaporize the tensions that can cause binges in the first place.

My program is not *the program*. That program does not exist. But the SOS approach is highly favorable for overeaters to fashion the program that suits them.

Using the SOS Meeting Structure

I would make the following suggestions for people with food problems—overeaters as well as bulemics, anorexics, and others—

who wish either to attend SOS meetings with alcoholics and other drug abusers or to start separate meetings.

Create your own food and behavior modification program— your own abstinence—but don't impose it on others. Consistent with the SOS emphasis on individual responsibility for recovery, group members should retain responsibility for decisions about their abstinence. Too many times we've been subjected to rigid, prefabricated diets that ignored our individuality, then been made to feel guilty and humiliated if we couldn't stick to them. Therefore, there should be no uniform SOS food or behavior program, no "official" SOS diet. Instead, SOS meetings can be a forum where individuals with food problems share their experiences about what works for them and discuss nutrition and eating behavior rationally and critically.

Start simply. Part of the appeal of a rigid program is that beginners can start at once. The drawback is that they can't progress. Since the SOS approach lacks hard structure, newcomers may have difficulty getting started. Some may feel they require a preset pattern. These individuals can consult a doctor or nutrition specialist, or adopt some food program that has worked for them in the past. But others may simply feel overwhelmed by the responsibility for making massive and complex changes in their eating and behavior. These people can begin with simple changes. A newcomer could decide to stop eating while watching television, or between meals, or in the car. He or she could swear off two or three foods that have triggered binges. Once started, the newcomer can set a time—one month, two months—and at the end of it, evaluate the effect of the changes and the desirability of further ones. This reassessment should continue periodically until the newcomer develops and fine-tunes a working personal program.

Take advantage of the group suppport of alcoholics and other drug abusers at SOS meetings. Despite the different problems, I strongly believe that people with food problems can benefit from these meetings. I was very fortunate to be warmly welcomed at the Los Angeles meetings I first attended, though for a long time I was the only overeater present. I found discussions on the difficulties of facing life without relying on my drug of choice to be particularly helpful, and I very much empathized with other people's struggle for recovery.

In areas with too few people for food-oriented SOS meetings, it is especially important that existing SOS meetings permit overeaters to attend. Many overeaters are desperate for secular group support, yet either lack the resources for commercial weight-loss programs or dislike their rigid diets. SOS can help these individuals, and the lack of overeater SOS meetings need not prevent them from obtaining the support they need.

Since I began a secular approach to recovery, my life has improved dramatically. I've lost 86 pounds and dropped down through eight dress sizes. I can now enjoy many kinds of physical activity. Small changes continue to excite and amaze me. My car doesn't always smell like food. I can actually stop when I've eaten enough and leave food on my plate. In the morning, I don't feel the bizarre mixture of nausea and intense hunger that comes from bingeing the night before. I've been able to maintain my self-respect and intellectual honesty through my recovery. I haven't had to surrender my rational, critical faculties to deal with my eating problems. Instead I've used them as allies. For me, it's been indispensable.

8. An Interview with John Lanagan

James Christoper

If there is one book likely to provoke profound changes in our perception of alcoholism and its treatment, it is *AA and the Alcoholic Beverage Industry* by John Lanagan. The author has agreed to discuss some of the information in the book, which is near completion and soon to be released. Lanagan is a researcher and freelance writer who specializes in addiction issues.

Q: You are an outspoken critic of Alcoholics Anonymous.

A: I'm not a malicious critic. But I'm not going to pretend all is well with AA when all is not well.

Q: Do you question AA's success?

A: AA is extremely successful. Unfortunately, this success has always been in public relations/publicity rather than overall treatment effectiveness. Maybe some day the media will show the negative side of AA, the people who have been harmed by this system. Alcoholics Anonymous is always portrayed as THE solution, and it is—for the alcoholic beverage industry. AA helps the industry far more than it has ever helped those addicted to alcohol.

Q: Your book, *AA and the Alcoholic Beverage Industry,* is an eye-opener. Even the most devout Alcoholics Anonymous folks are going to have to deal with some very disturbing revelations.

A: I hope so. I hope they have the courage to deal with it. For more than half a century AA has conveniently provided the alcoholic beverage industry with the illusion, rather than the reality, of overall effectiveness. The industry has been protected by this illusion. My book will show how AA serves the industry politically and economically; how AA's structure, traditions, teachings, and philosophy are so advantageous to the industry that they may as well have been designed by the industry itself.

Q: What does AA do for the industry?

A: AA serves the industry by politically neutralizing those who have historically been its most dangerous opponents. AA is a decoy, and man has always invented decoys as a means to an end. For instance, in her excellent book *The Incredible Journey of Lewis and Clark,* Rhoda Blumberg describes the Indians' use of decoys: "One Indian acting as a decoy covered his body with buffalo skin and wore a cap resembling a buffalo head. The decoy raced in front of a herd and headed for a cliff, while other Indians chased the herd from the rear, until the animals fell to their deaths. The Indian decoy jumped aside at the brink. If he wasn't quick enough he went over the cliff too." The Indians used their decoys to get food. Well, the industry uses AA as a decoy to sidetrack those who would otherwise present an economic and political threat. The buffalo, following the Indian decoy, thought they were being led to safety. In reality they were being sent to their deaths. Our nation thinks AA is the solution to alcoholism. In reality it is effective for only a segment of the alcoholic population, impedes strategies of abstinence and prevention, and hinders the implementation of more effective treatment methodologies. Yet alcoholics continue to be herded into AA.

Q: Interesting.

A: Horrifying. Here is why AA is invaluable to the industry:

1. The nation's alcoholics are channeled into the politically impotent, nonactivist AA religion, the traditions of which categorically forbid any organizational stand on issues relevant to alcoholism or its prevention. I have in my possession a letter from a former manager of AA's General Service Office that states, "We have no activities in prevention, research, education or treatment of alcoholism. . . . AA takes no position at all, either for or against warning labels on alcoholic beverages, nor on DWI legislation, nor on the 'fetal alcohol syndrome,' nor do we take any position on the general subject of drinking or not drinking alcohol."

Now, alcoholism and alcohol-related damages cost this nation $116 billion annually. Alcohol is frequently involved in suicides and violent behavior. Countless lives have been ruined, families destroyed. Alcohol has caused far more damage to our society than have cocaine and heroin combined. The people who should be doing the most to prevent others from becoming addicted are those who have become addicted themselves. But because the nation's alcoholics are funneled into the anti-activist AA movement, the industry has never had to worry about political repercussions from the very people who have been ravaged by the bottle. Thanks to AA, the industry doesn't have to worry about receiving criticism, bad publicity, or organized opposition from the nation's alcoholics.

2. Family members are channeled into Alanon, which has the same structure, traditions, and policy of noninvolvement. Family members are taught that alcoholism is caused by character defects, shortcomings, and so on. Never is alcohol itself seen as the culprit. Alanon's belief system virtually guarantees there will be no relatives seeking public forums to reveal how alcohol addiction destroyed a loved one. Because of Alanon there are no anti-alcohol family members going to the media, warning that drinking can indeed result in addiction; there are no family members organizing, uniting, seeking political solutions to the industry's ads aimed at young people; no family members demanding warning labels.

Before AA, many spouses and relatives of alcoholics were like wounded tigers. Having lost a loved one to the bottle, they joined the temperance movement determined to prevent the same thing from happening to other families. They were among the most savvy and dedicated of the temperance activists. Through Alanon these wounded tigers have been defanged. Through Alanon these wounded tigers have become house cats.

3. AA's religious structure encourages members to oppose and denigrate other, more effective and/or positive treatment methodologies. AA, ironically, while refusing to confront an industry that benefits economically from alcohol addiction, does everything in its members' power to denigrate and eliminate alternative treatments. Devout AA members see alternative treatments, rather than the industry's economic reliance on alcohol addiction, as offensive.

4. AA is a program of self-blame, and even, at its most extreme, a program of self-hate. AA teaches alcoholics that addiction is their own fault. "We reluctantly come to grips with those serious character flaws that made problem drinkers of us in the first place, flaws which must be dealt with to prevent a retreat into alcoholism once again." That's from "Twelve Steps and Twelve Traditions." If you are going to sell a product that will harm ten percent of those who use it, how do you want that product perceived? As dangerous? As addictive? That could tend to screw up sales. It did once before—this is what brought about Prohibition. But when the victims themselves are taught that alcoholism is the fault of the individual, marketing and advertising become so much easier.

5. AA is relatively ineffective but is perceived and portrayed as extremely effective. As AA co-founder Bill Wilson came to understand, AA works for just one motivated alcoholic in eighteen. From 1935 until 1955 Bill W. was trying to get all the nation's alcoholics into AA. But from 1955 until his death in 1971, he was engaged in a desperate search for more effective non-AA alternatives. Bill W. knew that most alcoholics simply cannot re-

spond to the Alcoholics Anonymous approach. But this is not what AA teaches. The "Big Book" tells alcoholics: "Rarely have we seen a person fail who has thoroughly followed our path." Alcoholics are taught that failure to attain sobriety via AA is due either to lack of motivation or dishonesty. Most AA members are intermittently sober. When they're sober they praise AA; when they relapse they blame themselves even as they buy more of the industry's products. Alcoholics, one-tenth of the drinking population, purchase half the alcoholic beverages sold annually. Rather than suggesting to those who have failed repeatedly via AA that perhaps another method should be tried, they are instead informed that AA remains their only possible hope. This is an economic bonanza for the industry. Their best customers, alcohol addicts, are trapped, recycled through a system that simply does not work for the majority of alcoholics.

Q: What is the nature of alcohol addiction?

A: Well, that's the thing. In over forty-one years of longitudinal and psychological studies, researchers have never found consistent evidence of the so-called "alcoholic personality." Alcoholics have many different personalities and many different personality traits, same as nonalcoholics. Alcoholics start out drinking for the same reasons everybody else does. The difference is, our bodies can't handle it. Researchers have once again linked alcoholism with genetics, but, fortunately for the industry, that's not AA's outlook. The "Big Book," the AA "bible," literally teaches, "Liquor is but a symptom."

Dr. James Milam sums up AA's understanding of alcoholism pretty well in his book *Under The Influence*. According to Milam, "AA stands as a colossal paradox. The fellowship has undoubtedly been the most powerful force in getting society to accept alcoholism as a treatable disease. Yet at the same time, it has become a powerful obstacle to accepting the otherwise overwhelming evidence that biological factors, not psychological or emotional factors, usher in the disease." This is why the industry loves AA and, for that matter, the new group, Rational Recovery. These groups essentially turn alcoholics on themselves. The substance itself is never even considered. RR is heavily influenced by controlled-drinking advocates, and controlled drinking—the alcoholic being taught to drink "correctly"—presupposes the drinker is at fault for not being able to drink socially in the first place. It is interesting that AA and RR, both of which teach that alcoholism is self-inflicted, receive massive publicity. If SOS, which understands the genetic underpinnings of the disease, were the recipient of such publicity, the industry would be in real trouble.

Q: Why?

A: When alcoholics en masse understand the genetic bases of the disease and are allowed to retain a positive image of themselves, the vast majority will become active in preventing others from becoming addicted. Prevention is where it's at. By that I mean abstinence. Those who do not drink are those who cannot become addicted. AA teaches that alcoholics can remain sober by helping one another. That is very true. But they can also remain sober by working to prevent addiction from happening to others.

Q: You think alcoholics and their families should stress prevention through abstinence?

A: Alcoholics and their loved ones have very good reason—maybe even a moral obligation—to work to prevent others from becoming addicted. I don't know about you, but my alcoholism was miserable. No one should have to go through hell like that. Those of us who have become addicted should be working like hell to let young people know what can happen to those who drink. But alcoholics and their families are not working for prevention. Alcoholics and their families don't get involved opposing things like alcohol industry ads targeted at young people, ads that glorify drinking. No, the industry's greatest potential opposition, the people who could really turn things around, have all been channeled into the 12-step movement. AA/Alanon run interference for the industry by politically emasculating this potentially very powerful pro-prevention lobby. AA's traditions forbid an organizational stand against the industry; AA further depoliticizes its converts by teaching that alcoholism is the fault of the alcoholic. Right now, between AA and RR, alcoholics and their families are docile and oh-so-malleable. Alcoholics who see the disease as genetic, who see alcohol as dangerous, are going to demand some controls on advertising. In 1990 retail sales of alcoholic beverages equaled $92 billion. Half of that, $46 billion, came from alcohol addicts, despite the fact that alcoholics constitute just one-tenth of the drinking population. The good news is that nonaddicted drinkers are continuing to cut down or quit entirely. The bad news is that, with social drinking on the downswing, alcoholics are more economically important to the industry than ever before. And so are Alcoholics Anonymous and Rational Recovery.

Q: Whom do you see as a potential political and economic hindrance to the industry?

A: Well, as mentioned, the families of alcoholics and alcoholics themselves. But also social activists. Abstinent religious groups. Priests and pastors who have grown weary of watching families dissolve because of the bottle. These are essentially the same people who brought the industry to its knees seven decades ago. Two things characterized the temperance movement, the men and women who legislated Prohibition into existence: They were savvy, political activists; and they saw alcohol itself as the problem. I'd like to quote researchers Reid Hester and William Miller, authors of the *Handbook of Alcoholism Treatment Approaches*: "The core assumption of the temperance model, whether or not directed toward prohibition, is that the cause of alcohol problems is alcohol itself. The drug is seen as so dangerous as to warrant great caution in use, if it is to be used at all. This is similar to the way in which drugs such as heroin and cocaine are currently viewed."

Q: But not alcohol?

A: Not alcohol. Not any longer. Hester and Miller also write:

"In 1933 the United States was in a conceptual quandary. The dominant view of alcohol problems had been that they were caused by the pernicious nature of alcohol itself. Yet the Congress had just voted to make alcohol freely available again, and a majority of states ratified it into law. A new model was needed. It was just two years later that Alcoholics Anonymous came into being, and with it was born the American disease model of alcoholism."

Q: So the people who brought on Prohibition saw alcohol itself as dangerous?

A: Yeah. Like our 12-step friends, the temperance people didn't see character defects as having anything to do with alcohol addiction. They saw the substance itself as dangerous. They were prevention oriented. Those who do not drink, they realized, are those who cannot become addicted. This is the same strategy we use with nicotine, cocaine, even AIDS. Stay safe through preventative measures. Don't put yourself in a position where it could become your problem.

Q: We don't do this with alcohol—stress prevention—yet at the same time we're trying to preempt addiction to cocaine by preventing its arrival on our shores. Strange.

A: One of many sad ironies where alcohol is concerned. When Prohibition ended in 1933, thirty-eight percent of the U.S. population still lived in areas that were dry by choice. The industry leaders had little love for the temperance activists. The industry had been legislated out of existence, forced to watch while gangsters ike Al Capone made fortunes. With the end of Prohibition a means had to be found to prevent any future resurgence of the temperance activists. AA, with its "disease-but-not-a-disease" understanding of alcoholism, has accomplished this.

According to the liquor industry's own literature, the industry "has helped to develop the concept of alcoholism as a disease, of which the excessive use of alcohol is a symptom but not the cause, and for which prohibition is not the answer." This strategy of changing our societal perception of alcohol and alcoholism has worked very well. Before AA, the families of alcoholics joined the temperance movement and worked very hard to prevent others from becoming addicted. Now they join Alanon, work on their own supposed character defects, and no longer see the substance as having caused the problem in the first place. Before AA, many priests and pastors stressed abstinence: "Don't drink and you cannot become addicted." Now clerics are essentially AA recruiters. They no longer see alcohol as addictive, they see alcoholism as "spiritual." They have been convinced that everything related to alcoholism should be handled by AA; that's the full extent of their involvement in the alcoholism field. Many religious people used to do one hell of a lot more than just hand over the victims to AA.

Q: Some people are not going to want to believe any of this, particularly the assertion that AA functions as a decoy for the industry.

A: The assertion is obvious. The only surprise is that it's taken this long to be pointed out. But I can understand how upset people are going to be.

Q: So what is your solution? Are you calling for a return to Prohibition?

A: No. There should be no return to Prohibition. But neither should we allow alcohol advertisements to be aimed at young people. These ads glorifying drinking never give a hint—not a glimmer—that one new drinker in ten will have trouble with alcohol. In my book I document just how pervasive the pressure is to drink, particularly in terms of the ads kids see over and over and over. Drinking is glorified, linked with beautiful women and good times and even, incredibly, sporting events. But when someone becomes addicted then it's "alcohol abuse." This may be an industry-originated term, by the way. According to Dr. James Milam, "Another example of the power of words to promote misconception is the use of the term 'alcohol abuse' as a synonym for 'alcoholism.' " Semantics can be very powerful. The industry tries to use the word "alcoholism" as little as possible. James Sanders of the Beer Institute recently lamented the "abusive use of our product." Again, this is why AA and RR are so valuable to the industry, because this is precisely what they teach.

Q: Where does Jean Kirkpatrick's group, Women For Sobriety, fit into all this?

A: Women For Sobriety, like SOS, is a danger point for the industry. WFS and SOS allow the alcoholic the gift of self-esteem. AA has essentially defanged the wounded tigers, turned the victims on themselves. But SOS, since it clearly understands the genetics underlying alcohol addiction, may be the birthplace for prevention-oriented alcohol activists.

Q: But SOS is not political.

A: No, but SOS respects intellect, the ability to think. The SOS newsletter takes on any subject, and SOS members are willing to discuss any issue. I predict that, once having read my book, many people will view alcohol, alcoholism, the industry, and Alcoholics Anonymous in terms of politics and economics. In this interview I am trying to speak more or less in generalities. In my book I will reveal specifics. People are going to be quite surprised about AA and the industry.

Q: Why have you chosen to reveal this now?

A: I wanted this to appear first in SOS Sobriety: The Proven Alternative to 12-Step Programs because SOS is a true grass-roots movement, quite similar to the Washingtonians, the original alcohol support group of the 1800s. SOS is secular, but religious people are made to feel very welcome. I've sent many there myself. Many Christians are of the view that AA is a religion, and they do not want to worship outside their own faith. SOS has been invaluable in this regard and I'm very appreciative of this. AA, by the way, has repeatedly been ruled a religion in the courts. SOS, full of believers and nonbelievers, is tolerant of diverse belief systems.

Q: SOS is about recovery. What a person believes or doesn't believe is secondary to overcoming alcoholism.

A: Yeah. Alcoholism should be treated like any other medical disease. Only AA and Christian Science treat disease with spirituality.

Q: What is your best-case scenario regarding alcoholism?

A: Alcohol will be seen as an addictive drug once again. AA will be one option among many. WFS and SOS will continue to grow. Aversion therapy, now used solely by Schick Hospitals, will be implemented on a national level. Aversion therapy has a documented seventy percent success rate. It worked for my dad. It worked for my godfather. It worked for the father of my best friend. And it worked for me. Our nation will come to understand that, despite AA's claims, there is no one, single way to get sober. Our country will also come to realize there is one sure way to prevent alcoholism in those genetically predisposed: prevention through abstinence. But it must also be understood that nine drinkers in ten are not genetically predisposed to alcoholism. People are going to drink. Hell, people have the right to drink. But the industry does not have the right to glorify alcohol in ads aimed at young people, not when it's a certainty that one new drinker in ten will become addicted. Rather than get rid of the industry, via a return to Prohibition, we need to dethrone Alcoholics Anonymous. Once AA is but one treatment option among many, abstinence will once again be used as a means of prevention. Once AA is dethroned, alcoholics will be able to gain access to more effective treatment methods. Let us be grateful for those AA has helped; but it's time to save the rest of us.

Q: How do you see things now?

A: The industry itself makes half its money from those addicted to its products. Alcoholics are cattle, existing primarily for the economic benefit of the industry; Alcoholics Anonymous is the stockyard we have been herded into; and our owner, in the big white house atop the hill, is the alcoholic beverage industry.

9. Alcoholics Anonymous and the United States Government: Some Constitutional Issues

James L. Monroe, Esq.

Often a person will enter an SOS meeting for the first or second time and use his or her initial opportunity to speak to vent anger verging on rage against Alcoholics Anonymous (AA). This anger may be misplaced, however, because AA is really a voluntary program and never forces anyone to join against their will.

In these cases of misplaced fury, resentment could usually be legitimately targeted at the judicial system, the treatment center, the individual therapist, or the alcohol program that sent this person to AA. Even though there is mounting evidence to the contrary, many treatment centers assure their charges that sobriety without AA is a miserable impossibility. Most treatment centers and alcohol programs in the country are staffed by AA members who see the goal of treatment as role rehearsal for AA participation.

One problem with these programs as well as judicially enforced AA participation is that they are explicitly forbidden by the First Amendment of the Constitution. A second problem arises because there is no corroborated research that supports the basic assumption that Alcoholics Anonymous is any more effective than any other method of abstinence. A third problem with the overwhelming adherence to AA principles in treatment settings has to do with the personal, psychological, and political aspects of teaching people that they have individual character defects that create susceptibility to a physical addiction to legal beverages that are widely available.

Mandated participation in AA and excessive treatment-center entanglement with AA are violations of the U.S. Constitution. This is not merely a matter of conjecture if one agrees that Alcoholics Anonymous is a religion.

Webster's Dictionary[1] defines religion as

1) Belief in a divine or superhuman power or powers to be obeyed and worshiped as the creator(s) and ruler(s) of the universe,

2) expression of this belief in conduct or ritual,

3) (a) any specific system of belief, worship, conduct, etc., often involving a code of ethics and a philosophy; as, the Christian religion, the Buddhist religion, etc.;

   (b) loosely, any system of beliefs, practices, ethical values, resembling, suggestive of, or likened to a system; as humanism[2] is his *religion,*

4) a state of mind or way of life expressing love for and trust in God, and one's will and effort to act according to the will of God. . . .

Certainly the practices of Alcoholics Anonymous are susceptible to interpretation as being a religious organization under any of the foregoing definitions. Even though AA insists upon a distinction between religious groups and a "spiritual program," the reality of the AA program makes any such distinction moot.

AA opens every meeting with a prayer to God (the "Serenity Prayer"[3]) and closes each meeting with a ritualistic holding of hands while reciting the Lord's Prayer. The 12 steps to recovery that are the explicit foundation of the program are replete with religious dogma. The second and third steps are "Came to believe that a power greater than ourselves could restore us to sanity"; and "Made a decision to turn our will and our lives over to the care of God as you understand Him."

The 9 steps that follow are ways to get in touch with the higher power and to reshape your life to conform to His will for you, culminating with an admonition to go out and "carry the message."

Some may insist that the allowance for a God "as you understand Him" somehow disclaims religiosity. A novitiate, however, soon learns that the God is Jesus and that one should keep a "good book next to the Big Book."[4] This is further confirmed by the program's development in 1935 from tenets of the Oxford movement, which followed the teachings of Dr. Frank Buchman, a Christian fundamentalist theologian.

Of course, *Webster's Dictionary* is not dispositive in regard to what the courts look to in enforcing the Establishment Clause of the First Amendment. It is included here as a reference on the assumption that we are dealing with generally accepted uses of the English language when we refer to religion. Semantic hocuspocus of substituting the word spiritual[5] for religious cannot make the true aspects of the program vanish nor can it change our fundamental understanding of what religion is.

Assuming that a lawsuit based upon constitutional grounds could convincingly characterize AA as a religion,[6] the plaintiffs would then be faced with showing that alcohol programs and judicial mandates violate the Establishment Clause.

Many people—including lawyers—have difficulty understanding the First Amendment[7] as an affirmative guarantee of freedom from religion. This clause was inserted to "prevent any national ecclesiastical establishment, which should give a hierarchy the exclusive patronage of the national government."[8]

Although the method for determining when and if an Establishment Clause violation has occurred seemed settled for many years, recent Supreme Court personnel changes leave all precedents in the area in doubt. The original test was established in 1971 by the Supreme Court in *Lemon* v. *Kurtzman*.[9] This *Lemon* test created three points to be examined in determining whether a government program violates the Establishment Clause.

First, a trier of fact should look for a secular purpose that the religion fulfills or that the government nexus with the religion may fulfill. In other words, is there a legitimate, nonreligious function served when one includes a religious viewpoint in a government program?

Here it is certainly true that AA referrals do serve the legitimate function of promoting a healthier society. However, the *Lemon* test requires that the program pass muster on both Part II and III as well as Part I. Part II requires that the government program not have the effect of advancing or endorsing any religion, and Part III forbids excessive entanglement between government and religion.

It will be impossible for treatment centers to tell the court that forcing people who are practicing Judaism, Buddhism, Hinduism, Islam, or atheism into a program that relies strictly on Jesus Christ for salvation from alcoholism does not advance Christianity over the other beliefs.

Finally, carting clients to and from the treatment centers to AA meetings, holding AA meetings at the centers, screening job applicants as to AA involvement by the treatment centers as well as the complicated procedures for monitoring AA attendance that the judicial system uses in sentencing and parole cases all rise above the standards of excessive entanglement set in previous Supreme Court cases.

Not only are most treatment programs administered by states and counties, but even privately funded programs receive Medicaid payments, are regulated by state governments, and are places to which public employees are sent by state and county medical-insurance carriers.

The common judicial practice of sentencing DWI (driving while intoxicated) and other penal code offenders to AA participation is in direct contravention with the holding in *Everson* v. *Board of Education.* This case states, "No person can be punished for entertaining or professing religious beliefs or disbeliefs, for church attendance or nonattendance." [10]

The punishment aspect in *Everson* occurs when a parolee or other person under sentence of law deigns to vary from the rigid constraints of the mandated AA attendance. In two recent federal district court cases the issue of court-mandated participation in Alcoholics Anonymous has come up. However, in both cases [11] the courts refused to respond to the issue of constitutionality. Both cases were deemed moot in regard to AA, because the defendants were no longer mandated to attend AA.

The mootness doctrine suggests to judges that they forego making decisions whenever the outcome of a case in question has been resolved prior to trial. This doctrine does not apply when the controversy in the case is likely to come up repeatedly. In these instances, and more that can be followed in other circuits, the issue of state-mandated participation in religious programs being a violation of the First Amendment is repeatedly called into controversy without resolution. The reluctance of these judges to decide on the constitutional question is typical, and it will be necessary for future litigants to bring in an ongoing or unresolved conflict.

Another barrier to suit on these grounds is a Supreme Court drifting perilously close to consistently rewriting all past interpretations of the First Amendment in favor of a notion of a "Christian nation." Recently Chief Justice Rehnquist wrote that it was all right for the city of Pawtucket to pay for, procure, and display the traditional Christian manger scene (creche) in the city square.

He wrote, "Based on the record in this case, the city has a secular purpose for including the creche in its Christmas display and has not impermissibly advanced religion or created an excessive entanglement between religion and government."[12]

Rehnquist went further, declaring that the Framers of the Constitution acknowledged a supreme being that looks over the country, that the Court would not, in the future, be constricted by following precedent such as the *Lemon* test.[13] It seems that activity on the high court may have a chilling effect on lower courts wanting to make forays into this part of the law that will ultimately be overturned.

Even though some of the founders, including Jefferson, believed in some type of Christian God, they realized that religion per se secured a peculiar type of control over the lives of individuals that was anathema to the concepts of a government based on democratic freedoms. Therefore, it was important to these men to insert a guarantee of freedom to practice the religion of one's choice as well as an explicit guarantee of the individual's freedom from religion.

By way of the Fourteenth Amendment to the Constitution, inserted after the Civil War, this guarantee of freedom from religion applies to all the states as well as the federal government. Case law from the past thirty years has extended the reach of this law to private enterprises that serve a traditional government function or that have a substantial nexus with government money or operations.

Therefore it would be quite reasonable for someone who was shunted into AA from a government-funded treatment program or through the sentence of a well-meaning judge to sue the state for injunctive relief. Additionally, the litigant should also prepare a permanent injunction to remedy the prevailing misuse of the treatment setting to promote the AA agenda.

Finally, Ellen Luff, an attorney with the Maryland ACLU (American Civil Liberties Union), has suggested that SOS attempt to write some legislation for incorporation in states to deal with problems such as this. This could be easily done based upon the legislation she has drafted for the Maryland legislature.

Introduced to the Maryland House of Delegates in February 1991, HB 542 states that it is offered

For the purpose of limiting the authority of a court to order a person as a condition of probation to participate in a rehabilitative program where religious or spiritual elements are an integral aspect of the program; and limiting the authority of an employer to require an employee to participate in rehabilitative programs where religious or spiritual elements are an integral aspect of the program.

Beyond the question of the best legal approach to remedy the inherent religious bias of most treatment programs lurks the serious scientific question of the true efficacy of sending people against their will into a religious milieu.

Where is the scientific research lending the weight necessary to hold the majority of people suffering from one of the most prevalent disorders of our time hostage to a single mode of treatment? Where is one credible iota of empirical evidence that God plays the most important role in getting straight?

In 1947 the founder of AA, Bill Wilson, wrote that AA and treatment centers should stay at arm's length in order that neither the AA name nor the medical profession become inexorably intertwined.

Briefly summarizing, I'm rather sure our policy with respect to "outside" projects will turn out to be this: A.A. does not sponsor projects in other fields. But, if these projects are constructive and noncontroversial in character, A.A. members are free to engage in them without criticism if they act as individuals only, and are careful of the A.A. name. Perhaps that's it. Shall we try it?[14]

However, in 1978 there seemed to be a policy shift. In an AA pamphlet entitled *A.A. and the Medical Profession*[15] there was an assertion that the entire medical profession has come to the singular conclusion that alcoholics need a personality change equal to a spiritual awakening. Further it states that Alcoholics Anonymous is a "cooperative meeting ground" for all the recognized tenets of medical treatment for alcoholism and the AA methodology.

Therein lies the problem with the common practice of staffing treatment facilities with AA members. Even though there are a plethora of treatment modalities that have varying degrees of acceptance and success, there is a nationwide tendency to forego research and stick to the majority modality. Further, follow-up to treatment usually consists of merely one phone call to an old address two months to a year after treatment to determine rate of "cure."

The 1984 *Report to Congress* concerning alcohol and drug abuse included the following excerpt from the National Reporting Program (NRP) in regard to patient outcome (read "recovery rate") for the state-run treatment facilities in the U.S.:

Although the NRP currently includes information on disposition of cases at termination (e.g. discharge or referral), it does not contain any data by which to assess the efficacy of treatment provided. In combination with information on sequential courses of treatment, data on patient outcomes would permit a better assessment of different types of treatment to improve patient management, as well as provide a minimum data base for use in research on organizational and staff effectiveness.[16]

Also in this treatise was a chart showing that sixty-two percent of treatment center clinicians have degrees and training categorized as "other" (listed under "2 Year UnderGrad, 4 Year UnderGrad, Master, and PhD.") or workshops as their credentials. Additionally, the report failed to state where the "referrals" were sent to after treatment. One can only speculate that these nondegree credentials were AA membership and that these referrals were generally to Alcoholics Anonymous.

Independent research on the long-term sobriety rates of alcoholics after treatment gives little or no indication that AA is a suitable outpatient program. A study in 1977 summarized AA as

[T]he oldest and most established of all treatment programs for alcoholism. It is an integral part of most treatment programs. Studies have found that A.A. members are most likely to be single, religiously oriented people who have lost drinking friends. Their wives and girlfriends support their A.A. participation. They are not highly symptomatic and are socially dependent, guilt prone persons with obsessive-compulsive and authoritarian personality features, prone to use rationalization and reaction formation. They are verbal persons who can share reaction with others and are not threatened by groups of people.

As a primary treatment method compared to alcohol clinic treatment, A.A. seems to be less successful. However, as a supplementary treatment program, A.A. may reach a wider audience. Physicians should recommend A.A. only to those people likely to profit from it.[17]

Apart from the structure of AA and the likelihood of certain personalities to assimilate looms the bigger question of whether the AA approach to abstinence is the most reliable. AA insists that only with a conversion experience can one see the light and become sane again. The AA brochure mentioned earlier is an example of the integration of the field of treatment with the AA perception that only deeply rooted psychological, emotional, or spiritual problems are the harbinger of the disease.

A group of British scientists studied one hundred married men who had voluntarily submitted to alcohol treatment in a controlled setting. The group found that directing the men toward AA enhanced the likelihood that they would join AA but did not enhance their chance of staying sober beyond the statistical norms.[18]

Similarly a California study found that

The relatively uniform rates of remission for different treatment modes, including Alcoholics Anonymous meetings, tend to contradict theories maintaining that alcoholism must be treated by dealing with deeper psychological problems. In fact, recovery from alcoholism may depend upon a mechanism quite unrelated to the factors that led to the onset of excessive drinking.[19]

Still, despite a growing number of outpatient and aftercare options for treatment centers, the vast majority remain steadfast in their refusal to attempt any other method.

SOS continually offers presentations to all interested treatment facilities, and many of these facilities do offer their staffs the opportunity to listen. Often during these presentations the presenter runs into open hostility from members of the treatment staff. Usually there is some attempt at prosecutorial cross-examination, with questions like "Well, if you have no 'program' how do you expect people to change their personalities?"

Detailed explanations of the assertion that a "personality change" is not necessarily the goal of a viable abstinence program may lead to a frustrating game of semantic football. Correspondingly, it is difficult to explain to someone entrenched in AA philosophy that merely staying off booze with support for self-empowerment is, in fact, a program and that all notions of personality change and "psychological healing" can be a separate issue.

This leads to a third concern about the legal and social implications of alcohol treatment dominated by AA. Not only is AA traditionally male dominated, but it also expressly teaches people that their own personal shortcomings are responsible for their disease. Even though AA scoffs at the notion that willpower alone can interrupt alcoholic behavior and calls alcoholism a disease, AA blames the victim by assuring him or her that the only method for recovery is to make a list of his or her shortcomings and make amends to all those he or she has hurt. This literally exonerates the manufacturers, advertisers, and purveyors of alcohol from any responsibility for its overuse.

AA also says that the first step to recovery is to admit that you are powerless over alcohol. This is a dubious political message because if believed it forces you to accept as gospel anything that the "program" tells you to do about your drinking. In other words, "you are not competent to stop drinking without our help and advice."

Interestingly, this disempowerment philosophy has led to a systematic, fatalistic approach to everything in life—one that is increasingly espoused by members and groups in AA. Two of the most popular bumper stickers in the program are "Turn It Over" and "Let Go and Let God." These are shortened ways of saying that whenever you have any type of problem, throw up your hands and ask God how to solve it or let God solve it.

Often a person at an AA discussion meeting will bring up a topic concerning some particular problem he or she is having with his or her spouse. As the people around the table take turns talking, complete strangers will give this person the most incredible advice based upon shop-worn truisms. Most of the advice leads to the inevitable conclusion that, regardless of the true nature of the problem, the person discussing it needs to be in better contact with his or her higher power.

Many times, for whatever real reason, disastrous consequences will befall the recipients of this advice. Rather than hearing anything resembling, "Maybe you can learn something positive from this experience," the unfortunate one will always hear, "Well, it was just God's will."

Irrespective of any personal belief systems, there is a dangerous assumption at work when an entire institution subscribes either implicitly or explicitly to such a disabling strategy. By virtue of the fact that most centers employ AA paraprofessionals and refer clients almost exclusively to AA, these centers are inherently adopting the disempowerment philosophy. This philosophy is contradictory, unscientific, and anathema to many peoples' well-thought-out personal belief systems.

All treatment programs and institutions having any nexus

whatsoever with government funding need to be scrutinized carefully so that it is clear what messages are being sent to people who are forced to use these facilities. The relationship between the professional staffs and the AA hangers-on[20] and hired counselors with AA credentials needs to be examined as well.

E. M. Patterson writes, in the *American Journal of Psychiatry,* that, "The negativistic attitudes of professionals remains a major obstacle to effective treatment. Establishing an effective working collaboration between professionals and paraprofessionals is a new challenge in the field of treatment. The field is currently dominated by paraprofessionals who use a base of 'folk science' contrasted to professionals who approach alcoholism from a base of 'academic' science."[21]

It seems that there should be a place in the treatment setting for those who by whatever means have gotten sober and stayed sober without remission for a significant amount of time. These persons with long-term sobriety have a lot to contribute: they make very effective role models with or without degrees in psychology or medicine. However, the problem is not really professional versus paraprofessional.

What is really missing is a widely available, open-minded approach to alcohol treatment that allows for individual differences and examines evidence with an eye toward improving on the conventional wisdom. If this were being done, there would be no need for the lawsuits that SOS envisions will be necessary to remedy the current injustices.

Notes

1. Jean L. McKechnie, ed., *Webster's Deluxe Unabridged Dictionary,* 2d ed. (New York: Shuster and Shuster, 1979), p. 1527.

2. SOS does not promote humanism or any other philosophical viewpoint as a prerequisite to sobriety.

3. "God grant me the Serenity to accept the things I cannot change; the Courage to change the things I can; and the Wisdom to know the difference."

4. *The Bible and Alcoholics Anonymous* by Bill Wilson (1935)—usually referred to as the "Big Book" in AA.

5. Defined in *Webster's* as "5) of religion or the church; sacred, devotional, or ecclesiastical; not lay or temporal." McKechnie, *Webster's*, p. 1751.

6. Putting aside for the moment the very real questions of standing, and possible injunctive relief to be sought.

7. U.S.C.A. Const. Amend. 1. "Congress shall make no law respecting an establishment of religion or prohibiting the free exercise thereof; or abridging the freedom of speech, or of the press; or the right of the people peaceably to assemble, and to petition the Government for a redress of grievances."

8. 3 Story, *Commentaries on the Constitution of the United States* 728 (1833).

9. 403 U.S. 602 (1971).

10. 330 U.S. 1 at 16.

11. Sheldon v. Edgar, 475 N.E.2d 956 (Ill. A.D., 1985), an Illinois DWI case; and, Farmer v. Coughlin, 1987 WL 27664 (SD NY), a New York parole-violation case.

12. Lynch v. Donnelly, 104 S.Ct. 1355 (1984) at 1361.

13. Note, "Religious Social Service Providers," 75 Virginia Law Review 1077, 1989.

14. Bill Wilson: *A.A. Tradition; How it Developed,* pamphlet of Alcoholics Anonymous World Services, 1947, p. 22.

15. General Services Corp.; Alcoholics Anonymous World Services, 1978, p. 10.

16. Public Health Service, *Alcohol and Drug Abuse and Mental Health Services Data, Report to Congress,* January 1984. Published by U.S. Department of Health and Human Services, Alcohol, Drug Abuse, and Mental Health Administration, pp. 4–27.

17. F. Buckland, "Evolution of Treatment Methods in Chronic Alcoholism," *Treatment and Rehabilitation of the Chronic Alcoholic* (New York: Plenum Press, 1979), pp. 385–440.

18. G. Edwards, J. Orford, et al., "Alcoholism: A Controlled Trial of Treatment and Advice," *Journal of Studies on Alcohol* 38, no. 5 (1977): 1004–31.

19. D. J. Armor, J. M. Polich, and H. B. Stanbul, *Alcoholism and Treatment* (Santa Monica, Calif.: Rand Publishing, 1976).

20. It is common for treatment centers to offer their facilities to AA groups for regularly scheduled meetings. The outcome of this practice is a reliance by the treatment centers on the "expertise" of the participating AA members, as well as the elevation of the organizers and chairman of the meetings to authority figure status. Many times these relationships develop over many years, and certain AA members become "fixtures" at these state-run institutions.

21. E. M. Patterson, "Ten Years of Change in Alcoholism Treatment and Delivery Systems," *American Journal of Psychiatry* 134, no. 3 (1977): 261–66.

Select Bibliography

Blum, Kenneth, Ph.D., and James E. Payne. *Alcohol and the Addictive Brain.* New York: Macmillan Publishing, The Free Press, 1991.

Bufe, Charles. *Alcoholics Anonymous: Cult or Cure?* San Francisco: See Sharp Press, 1991.

Burns, David D., M.D. *Feeling Good: The New Mood Therapy.* New York: NAL Penguin, Inc., Signet Books, n.d..

Christopher, James. *How to Stay Sober: Recovery without Religion.* Buffalo, N.Y.: Prometheus Books, 1988.

———. *Unhooked: Staying Sober and Drug Free.* Buffalo, N.Y.: Prometheus Books, 1989.

Fitzgerald, Kathleen Whelan, Ph.D. *Alcoholism: The Genetic Inheritance.* New York: Bantam Doubleday Dell Publishing Group, Doubleday, n.d.

Goodwin, Donald W., M.D. *Is Alcoholism Hereditary?* New York: Oxford University Press, 1976.

Israel, Yedy, and Jorge Mardone. *Biological Basis of Alcoholism.* New York: John Wiley & Sons, Wiley-Interscience, 1971.

Jellinek, E. M. *The Disease Concept of Alcoholism.* New Haven, Conn.: College and University Press; and New Brunswick, N.J.: Hillhouse Press, 1960.

Kasl, Charlotte Davis, Ph.D. *Many Roads, One Journey: Moving Beyond the Twelve Steps.* New York: Harper Perennial, A Division of HarperCollins Publishers, 1992.

Milam, James R., and Katherine Ketcham. *Under the Influence: A Guide to the Myths and Realities of Alcoholism.* New York: Bantam Books, n.d..

Smith, James W., M.D., and Joseph Frawley, M.D. "Long-Term Abstinence from Alcohol in Patients Receiving Aversion Therapy as Part of a Multimodal Inpatient Program." *Journal of Substance Abuse Treatment* 7: 77–82. (Drs. Smith and Frawley are affiliated with Schick Health Services, Seattle, Washington, and Shadel Hospital, Santa Barbara, California. This study was published by Permagon Press.)

Vaillant, George E., M.D. *The Natural History of Alcoholism: Causes, Patterns, and Paths to Recovery.* Cambridge, Mass.: Harvard University Press, 1983.

For further information, contact:

Secular Organizations for Sobriety/Save Our Selves
SOS International Clearinghouse
Post Office Box 5
Buffalo, NY 14215-0005
(716) 834-2922

Contributors

KENNETH BLUM, Ph.D., an internationally recognized authority on psychopharmacology and substance abuse, is professor of pharmacology, Chief of the Division of Addictive Diseases, and Director of the Laboratory of Pharmacogenetics at the University of Texas Health Science Center at San Antonio.

GERARD J. CONNORS is a senior researcher at the Research Institute on Addictions, Buffalo, New York.

KAREN E. COURCHAINE is a doctoral student in counseling psychology in the Graduate School of Education, Kent State University, Kent, Ohio.

KURT H. DERMEN is a researcher at the Research Institute on Addictions, Buffalo, New York.

MARK DUERR is a researcher at the Research Institute on Addictions, Buffalo, New York.

ROSALIND GOLD, Esq., is an attorney and administrator who lives in Southern California.

JOHN LANAGAN is a researcher, writer, and lecturer living in Oregon.

WILLIAM M. LONDON is assistant professor of health education in the Graduate School of Education, Kent State University, Kent, Ohio.

JAMES L. MONROE, Esq., is an attorney practicing law in Niagara Falls, New York.

RICHARD SMITH is a retired airline executive living in Western New York.

SUSAN E. SMITH, M.A., conducts research in human resources and is the author of *Fear of Freedom: A Woman's Options in Social Survival and Physical Defense.*

DAVID L. YOHO recently completed his Ed.S. Degree in community counseling in the Graduate School of Education, Kent State University, Kent, Ohio.